Billy

The Life and Photographs of William S.A. Beal

For
Tom Barrow, Sr., Clifford Hanson and George Hunt, Sr.

The true art of memory is the art of attention.
—Samuel Johnson

Vig. Corps Press
558 Prosper Street
Winnipeg, Manitoba.
R2J 0M9

Cover Design by David Hopper

Book Design and Layout by Robert Barrow and Leigh Hambly

Typesetting by Triad Graphics Limited

ISBN 0-9693693-0-1

Printed in Canada by Friesen Printers

Table of Contents

Preface

I have a vivid memory from when I was about five years old. I remember standing with my father and a neighbour on the fairgrounds in Swan River. There were four Black men—I believe they were performers at the rodeo that year—standing in front of one of the booths. I remember the neighbour saying to my father that he thought they were White men appearing in black-face because, he said, the palms of their hands were white. I was staring intently at them, wondering if it could be true. Then my father said that, no, they weren't White. He talked about the Black people he had met when he went to Mississippi and then he said—Billy Beal's hands are like that.

That is the first time I recall hearing of Mr. Beal. I never met him. And although I have heard stories about him all my life, it was not until 1978 that I began to realize what an amazing man he had been. It was in that year that my father gave me eight of Mr. Beal's original glass negatives and asked me to make prints from them.

The quality of the plates and the sense of *a time* in them were superb. I began talking to people about Mr. Beal and by 1983, when I did the first interviews, I had located 72 of his glass plates. It was not until 1985, however, when Leigh Hambly and I agreed to work together on a publication, that the research began in earnest. In 1986, we applied for and were granted funding for research through the Explorations Program. This enabled us to complete the interviews with Mr. Beal's contemporaries, obtain records from various sources in Canada and hire researchers in the United States. Through all our efforts, we were supported by the people of the Big Woody district who had known Mr. Beal and who felt his was a remarkable life that should be recorded. We completed the first draft in 1987.

Our rejection slips were in sharp contrast to the excitement and support of everyone who heard of the project, saw Mr. Beal's photographs or read the manuscript. It was with this interest and encouragement that we determined to publish the book ourselves. We sincerely hope that the publication reflects the quality of that support and urge anyone who is interested in learning more of the history of Blacks in Canada to refer to the books in the Suggested Reading list.

Robert Barrow
September 1988

Foreword

The first section of this book is a short biography of William S.A. Beal, a Black American who settled in the Big Woody district northwest of Swan River, Manitoba circa 1905. Beal came out to work as a steam engine operator and machinist but dabbled quite expertly in several very diverse fields—furniture making, astronomy, philosophy, religion, medicine and photography. A Black man in a White society, he was a curiosity from the outset and became a myth in his own day. The second section of this book is a series of thumb nail sketches of people, events and activities in the Big Woody district as seen through Beal's photographs and the personal recollections of his acquaintances in the community.

The historical research, the collection of photos, the oral history interviews and the compilation of the text for this volume are the work of Robert Barrow and Leigh Hambly. Barrow, a native son of the Swan River area, is a photographer by profession. He has done archival photography, as well as numerous photo documentary projects and artistic work which have been exhibited and published widely including a recent Swan River photo exhibit entitled *Rural Route*. Hambly is an anthropology and history graduate who is currently developing a writing career. She has worked as a copy editor for heritage publications and has been published in magazines.

The biography of Beal is thoroughly researched relying on exhaustive tracing of all the threads of his background—his family antecedents in Massachusetts and Minnesota, his homestead records, his letters and local school and municipal history documents. A wider context is provided by a study of local histories of the area and the province, the geography of prairie settlement and relevant facets of Black history on this continent. This material is given human depth by the use of 20 oral history interviews with some of Beal's photo subjects as well as other key informants from the neighbourhood. They elaborate on Beal's inimitable character, give a first hand description of each photo in the volume and provide an impressionistic overview of a fascinating pioneer community.

Taken together, the historical narrative, photographs and excerpts of voices create an intimacy, realism and factual credibility that is rarely achieved in a local history. They depict a convivial multi-ethnic community of British, Eastern Canadian, American, Icelandic, Swedish and other peoples. Among them, Beal found a comfortable niche despite his racial background. He himself obviously contributed to the civility of that community.

Billy Beal is portrayed warmly but honestly showing his admirable qualities—so widely affirmed by his acquaintances—as well as some of his quirks and lapses of character. His plight as a member of a visible minority is dealt with in a sensitive but matter-of-fact fashion without pathos or moralistic commentary. As such, it provides a very meaningful insight into the missed opportunities, the unfair racial stereotypes, the stoic forebearance and the very real achievements of the man. It also shows the genuine openness that was extended to him by the community as they got to know him.

This book provides very entertaining reading, some captivating photo insights into a prairie community and a valuable historical documentary.

Steve Prystupa
Curator of Multicultural Studies
Manitoba Museum of Man and Nature
September 1988

Photographic Commentary

Photographs do not exist for us to only look once and to then become forgetful. Photographs do not rush by us like film for they have a permanence and a claim on us that cannot be diminished. For example, if one were to recall the major historical works of such photographers as Andre Kertesz or Henri Cartier-Bresson or Brassai, particularly images of war, famine or humanity, it is the image we remember more than the factual accounts of historians' analyses of an era.

This is what the best photographers are able to achieve. They take voyages and pull us with them to observe and experience pain and generosity or turmoil and dignity. More than any other characteristic, photographs offer the best vehicle for communicative exchange at the same time as they maintain a certain mystery. A single photograph may not give us the beginning or end of a story, reasons or explanations, but it does offer an intimate exchange with the viewer and contrasts between other peoples' lives and our own.

Viewing William Beal's photographs of the people and life in the Swan River Valley during the early twentieth century brings to mind all of the above attributes of photographic power. Beal's technique has cut across some established distinctions and borders in documentary photography and draws out actuality of location and people, the essential description of a place called Swan River. Beal may not have been consciously concerned with the "aesthetic" nature of documentary photography (as we know it today), but he did advance a model of documentary which avoids realist fallacy. Underpinning both document and comment is the virtue of Beal's work. In his strict and disciplined compositions, he has seen, understood, empathized and commented all the while as he identified himself with the people and events of a unique place that he called 'home'.

Generally speaking, the documentary tradition in photography evolved to include notions of evidence and instruction. It carried the record of external reality and forwarded obtained data for social transmission. Documentary work was considered objective and concerned with the presentation of social and historical situations and events in which the marks of the creator were secondary to the information itself. This cannot be said of Beal's approach for his subject matter was centrally concerned with his own sensibility.

Beal's assertions are true and sincere. The way to interpret these images seems not to be in reestablishing boundaries, which at best are difficult to articulate and in practice impossible to enforce, but to locate their meaning by understanding the images themselves—the stylistic and formal characteristics as well as the intrinsic meanings of the content—learning about the photographer's intentions and comprehending the cultural, historical and ideological context in which the photographs were taken...

so that the people of Swan River and us will not forget...

Shirley J.-R. Madill
Winnipeg, August 1988

Chapter One

Introduction

Mr. Beal read the books of philosophers. He read the writings of Spinoza. Have you ever read Spinoza? I know I haven't. [1]

On March 1, 1912, ten ratepayers from the Big Woody area, about 12 miles northwest of the townsite of Swan River, Manitoba, gathered at the home of Gus Jonsson to discuss the formation of a new school district. Although there were already several schoolhouses scattered throughout the Swan River Valley, the closest was still too far away for the many children now living in Big Woody to attend. When the meeting adjourned, the ratepayers—acting on behalf of concerned parents who wanted their children to have an education—had defined their intent and drawn up a petition to be presented to the council of the municipality. [2]

Recording the minutes of the meeting was 38-year-old William Beal. Three months later, when the ratepayers met again, he was elected a trustee and appointed Secretary-Treasurer of the Board of Trustees. For the next year and a half, until the Big Woody School opened its doors to its first pupils, he played an integral role in the formation of Big Woody School District #1621.

Billy, as he was known to his friends, had a keen interest in learning. Although he was a bachelor, he possessed a deep-rooted belief in the education of children—perhaps because of the opportunites not afforded him when he was growing up.

In the late 1890s, the Canadian and provincial governments unveiled a long, extensive advertising campaign to attract American farmers onto the Prairies. No mention was made of racial restrictions, and they did not foresee that many of those who would respond would be Black. Nor did they anticipate the wave of anti-Black sentiment that would sweep the Prairies as a result of this northern migration. According to Robin W. Winks in *The Blacks in Canada: A History,* the reaction of most

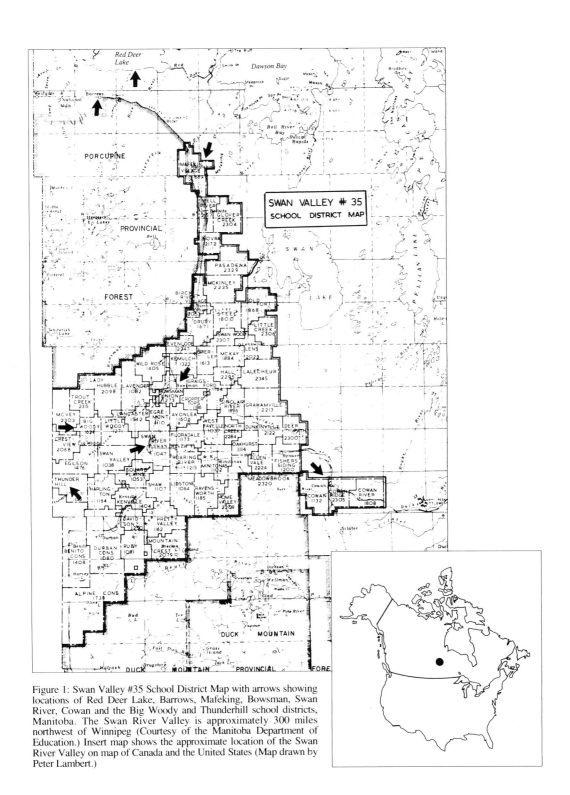

Figure 1: Swan Valley #35 School District Map with arrows showing locations of Red Deer Lake, Barrows, Mafeking, Bowsman, Swan River, Cowan and the Big Woody and Thunderhill school districts, Manitoba. The Swan River Valley is approximately 300 miles northwest of Winnipeg (Courtesy of the Manitoba Department of Education.) Insert map shows the approximate location of the Swan River Valley on map of Canada and the United States (Map drawn by Peter Lambert.)

Canadians to the immigration of Blacks was that "one or two...Negroes were a romantic curiosity; a hundred were a 'racial menace'." By the time Billy Beal arrived in the Swan River Valley, circa 1906, this racist attitude was being reinforced by the popular literature of the day—literature that tended to stereotype Blacks as "crafty...lazy, child-like and ignorant."[3]

Manitoba, despite its population of diverse cultural backgrounds, was not free of racism. In March 1911, for example, customs officers subjected a group of about 200 Black farmers from Oklahoma to a "most rigorous examination" upon their arrival at the international border-crossing at Emerson, Manitoba. The immigrants all met the necessary requirements for entry, however, and the officials—much to their chagrin—could not prevent them from coming into Canada.[4] That same year, citizens from several cities in western Canada, including Winnipeg, petitioned the federal government to halt the movement of Blacks onto the Prairies.[5] They had nothing to worry about; the federal government implemented a policy whereby border guards could stop Blacks, and other immigrants deemed as undesireable, from entering the country by declaring them as medically unfit. Applicants who were denied entry for medical reasons could not appeal the decision.

Despite such blatant and commonplace occurrences of racism, Billy Beal was, it seems, accepted by the people of the Swan River Valley. There is little—on the surface at least—to suggest that he was treated any differently than anyone else who settled in the area. Perhaps it was because, as the only Black for miles around, he was not a "racial menace" to the White settlers in the Valley. But a curiosity he was! He packed a pistol—though nobody recalls him ever firing it. He was a steam engineer, a skilled carpenter, an electrician and a photographer. He had a working knowledge of medicine and chemistry and, it is said, was well versed in the law. He was also learned and spoke with confidence on subjects as diverse as philosophy, religion, politics and astronomy: "Christ—he could tell ya every star in the sky!"[6]

Another curious thing about Billy was his claim that he was descended of White parents! Or was it only his father who was White? His mother? Nobody really seems to remember: "I think his mother was White. He told—he used to talk about it and I'm sure he said his mother was White."[7] And: "I'm almost positive that he had mentioned one time that either his father or mother was White and he had two sisters. He told us—he said they were as White as he was dark."[8] Regardless of what he actually told people, he never did reveal much information about himself; the diversity of the speculation on his origins more than made up for his own vagueness. As one resident of the Valley said, "In them days you never really delved into anybody's past. Rumours followed ya, but that's as far as it went."[9]

And there is no question that rumours followed Billy:

Well, he was a—he had Negro blood in him and it really came out in him, and his family, I guess, persuaded him to come up to this country so they wouldn't be embarrassed having this fella who showed so much Negro in the family.[10]

His father was a slave-owner and his mother was one of the slaves. The family was all White. They just sent him out of the country. They sent him away, that's all.[11]

They were White people but they had been of Negro blood and he turned out to be a Black one. And the other children were sort of—pretty well—White. And he turned out Black. He was a throwback and, of course, they didn't want to have anything to do with him... He just left them—to hell with them—and come up here.[12]

He was the only [Black] one here and we never could find out why he left [home]. And then we got to thinkin' maybe it was because—used to be slaves, you know. He didn't want to be a slave. And that was right in England....[13]

Mr. Beal told my father that he was born of White parents and was the seventh child of the seventh generation in which there was a colored relative.[14]

Where Billy came from, why he came to the Valley, who he really was—throughout his life, he kept the answers to himself. There was, however, one thing about Billy that everybody found out about soon enough. He was not a farmer. Still, this did not stop him from applying for his homestead entry a few years after he moved to the Swan River Valley.

1. Mervyn Minish speaking at the opening of the new Big Woody Hall, Big Woody district, Swan River, Manitoba, 1 July 1986.

2. Big Woody (Manitoba) School, Minutes of meeting of ratepayers to form a new school district. Meeting of 1 March 1912. *Note:* Imperial measurements are used throughout this publication in order to provide continuity with the measurements recorded in historical documentations and used by the people interviewed.

3. Colin A.Thomson, *Blacks in Deep Snow: Black Pioneers in Canada* (Don Mills:J.M.Dent & Sons, Canada Limited,1979),p.89.

4. Robin W. Winks, *The Blacks in Canada: A History* (Montreal:McGill-Queen's University Press,1977),p.308.

5. Thomson,p.102.

6. Interview with Clifford and Edie Hanson, August 1986.

7. Interview with Albert and Annie Daum, March 1986.

8. Interview with Vera Kennedy, June 1986.

9. Interview with George Fierstine, May 1986.

10. Interview with Tom, Sr. and Mary Barrow, December 1983.

11. Interview with Clifford and Edie Hanson, December 1983.
12. Interview with Inga Einarson, December 1983.
13. Interview with Lizzie Woolford, July 1986.
14. Letter from Beulah Vetters, 20 January 1986.

Chapter Two

Homesteading

...ten acres should be broken to earn a patent—this would equal 30 acres on cleaner land—Evidence of neighbours: The homesteader took his mother to Ontario to die. Woman now dead and the entrant is on his way back to improve his farm. Should be protected.[1]

If the people of the Big Woody district were awed by Billy Beal's extensive knowledge, talents and skills, they were also probably somewhat bemused by his ineptness as a homesteader and his indifference to his holdings. Clearing land and working the fields were not Billy's forte: "He was always using his head instead of his hands—his arms an' hands."[2]

Billy, it has been said, could not even grow a garden, let alone a field of wheat! But he tried. Of his first garden, which he planted in 1912, he commented, "I was very proud of my effort with my first experience but we had a frost every month that summer and I got nothing but the potatoes."[3]

It is questionable, however, whether the garden's failure was the result of the frost or Billy's own apathy; Billy "wasn't too ambitious as far as physical doin'."[4] One neighbour said, "His garden never amounted to anything." And recalling Billy's characteristic dry wit, added, "He always said he was waitin' for the [garden] stuff to get ahead of the weeds... I never knew him to get anything out of his garden."[5]

His few half-hearted attempts at farming were no more successful. He cleared just a "little patch of field, the rest was all bush and scrub"[6] and planted crops only until he received his "patent". No one remembers him ever earning—or trying to earn—any money from cropping his land or raising livestock. And on those occasions when he joined the threshing crews, his incompetence often spelled near disaster. One neighbour, recalling a time they were both working on the same crew, said:

> It was our team [of horses] that run away from him. It was an old team that we
> could never get any speed out of... I can remember we were threshin' there one
> night. It was just gettin' dark and I seen [the team of horses] comin' down the
> field, and they went by the machine and Beal had ahold of the back of the rack
> with one hand and a fork in the other hand and he was takin' steps about 20 feet
> long... He was on the ground leading the rack, you see, but he'd stick a fork in
> the horses [to get them to move forward]. That's why they took off, I guess.[7]

Farming may have been one of the few things Billy was not good at. But then
he preferred to live day-to-day: "And he never had a woodpile, you know. He'd just
go out in the morning, or whenever he got up—at noon or whatever—go out and
cut a tree and that was his wood supply."[8] Sometimes, however, his nonchalance,
particularly with regards to his physical comfort and safety baffled his friends. There
is, for example, the story of the time a neighbour, George Hunt, Sr., dropped in to
see him one winter morning, the temperature about minus thirty degrees Fahrenheit:

> ...[George] rapped on the door and Billy was still in bed and he said, "Come
> in." And the fire was out and it was cold in there and George said, "Never mind,
> stay in bed and I'll light the fire." And [Billy] said, "Yea, but there's no wood in
> the house." George said, "Well, I'll go out and get some," and Billy said, "Well,
> there's none cut." So, George had to go out [to the bush] and cut this wood and
> bring it in and light the fire... Later, George says, "Imagine a man going to bed in
> the middle of winter without even a stick of wood in the house... Just imagine a
> man being that content."[9]

Most of the homesteaders accepted, but did not fully understand, Billy's easygo-
ing approach to life on the frontier. Their dreams of making a quick fortune off the
cheap land, or of owning a piece of land—often for the first time— were not his
dreams. Billy had not come to the Swan River Valley with the intention of taking
out a homestead. Most had.

The fertile soils of the Valley had been noted by travellers through the region as
early as the 1850s. A series of political manoeuvres and continent-wide economic
crises, combined with the Valley's inaccessibility, shelved any plans to open up the
area to settlers until the 1880s.[10]

During the early 1880s, the political and economic climates had stabilized na-
tion-wide and, in Manitoba, the quest for settlers began. Aggressive advertising cam-
paigns—aimed primarily at farmers in Ontario and, to a lesser extent, farmers in the
United States—were launched by railway and shipping lines, land companies and
the Manitoban and Dominion governments. The campaign was so successful that,
by the end of the decade, filing for a homestead near existing settlements was next

to impossible. Clearly, new areas had to be opened up. The Swan River Valley was the obvious choice.

In 1889, the Lake Manitoba Railway and Canal Company, a small local enterprise, was chartered to build a rail line through the Valley.[11] The following year, though, the country was again in the throes of a depression and railway construction was halted everywhere for lack of funds.[12] By 1895, economic conditions had improved enough to resume construction of branch lines and, in late 1896, the railway was completed to Dauphin, Manitoba, about 100 miles south of the Swan River Valley.[13]

The first rush of homesteaders arrived in the Dauphin area early in 1898, a year after the Canadian and provincial governments began a new advertising campaign aimed specifically at American farmers. Some came by train, others by wagon. But if the trip up to Dauphin was long and hard, the journey still ahead, into the Swan River Valley, was even more difficult. These pioneers had come in along the "colonization" trail, also known as the Cowan Trail—a slashed road over the Duck Mountains and through muskeg—by foot, oxen and wagon, or horseback:

> [My father] came in 1898. There were some people here before that, you know—
> a year before—but everything was wild, you know, pretty well. No roads. Just
> had to ford the rivers and things like that... [My father] drove his horses and he
> had a wagon... And, I guess, they had to ford the rivers and so on. It wouldn't be
> very nice, I wouldn't think.[14]

Once they reached the end of the trail, they arrived at a make-shift settlement called Tent Town. Here, the settlers were greeted by Hugh Harley, a government land agent, who received and recorded homestead entries and distributed maps of the area.[15]

In the fall of 1899, the first train pulled into the town-site of Swan River. Within a matter of weeks, Tent Town was totally dismantled. Over 400 settlers were already in the Valley.[16]

The Minneapolis-St.Paul, Minnesota area was one of the regions where the Manitoba Government focussed much of its advertising. In 1901, for example, the *Saint Paul Broadax,* a newspaper for Blacks, printed articles in which Manitoba's Premier, R.P. Roblin, invited its readers to migrate north.[17]

It is possible, then, that Billy Beal, who was living in Minneapolis at the turn of the century, read the advertisements in the *Broadax* or another local newspaper. It is more probable, though, that he came to his homestead by a more circuitous route. In his memoirs, he writes,"I came to this country during Laurier's land boom... I did not come to this part of the country to homestead then but to follow my trade of engineer as there [were] many saw mills being opperated [sic]."[18]

The Swan River Valley, with its rich farmland, had not only become home to several thousand homesteaders by this time, but numerous lumber companies had opened mills in the area to take advantage of the thick, timbered forests and many natural waterways. Billy had been working at a sawmill in Minneapolis in various capacities.[19] Since many American firms had branches or subsidiaries in Canada, he may have lined up work at one of the mills prior to his arrival; during the summer of 1906 he was working as a steam engineer at one of the sawmills in the Valley.[20]

That fall, a friend he had met at the mill invited him to spend the winter with him on his homestead in the Lancaster district, "We went out there to fix up the house and things because he had a wife to share is [sic] good fortune with him. The scrub was so dence [sic] out there that we had to climb a tree to see much of his posessions [sic]."[21] Little wonder that he later remarked, "I had originally come from the city and I thought a man must have an awfull grug [sic] against a woman to take her out in the woods like that."[22]

Over the winter, though, he was struck by the community spirit of the people around him and decided it was "not so bad when one got used to it."[23] The sense of belonging and all the homestead talk in the sawmill bunkhouses convinced him, in 1908, to try his own hand at homesteading. On October 6, he applied for entry in Big Woody on SE 1/4 1-37-29.[24]

Legislative provisions, laid out in the Dominion Lands Act and administered by the Department of the Interior, provided homesteaders with several ways to obtain land. In the Big Woody area, a settler was usually given three years to "prove up" his land; that is, clear 30 acres, or fence his land and keep 30 head of livestock before he could apply for ownership or "patent". He also had to build a house and barn and reside on his land for six months of the year. Further, only entrants who were British subjects by birth or by naturalization could be issued patents.[25]

Billy's choice of a homestead was within a half mile of Gus Jonsson's, whose acquaintance he had made while working at the sawmill (Figure 2). Gus was a Swedish sailor who, after having jumped ship in Montreal and hiding in a brickyard to escape the authorities, had come west to seek his fortune.[26] That Gus never let the truth stand in the way of a good tale does cast some doubt as to the validity of this story.

Billy and Gus quickly became close friends—they were single, of the same age, facing the hardships of homesteading, and neither had much of an affinity for animals. When Billy said, "One of my oxen died and my next neighbor lost one ox too so we made a team of my remaining ox and his and worked that way,"[27] the

Figure 2: Crew in front of sawmill with Gus Jonsson(third from left)and William Beal(fifth from left, on log), Mafeking, Manitoba. c.1910. Photograph by Walter Barrie (Courtesy of Western Canada Pictorial Index/Swan Valley Museum Collection.)

neighbour he was referring to was probably Gus. Both men, it seems, lost most of their livestock due to neglect and maltreatment. Said one neighbour, "The only thing I had against [Billy]—and old Gus—was their goddamn meanness to animals."[28] They were an odd pair. Billy was quiet, polite and even-tempered; on the few occasions that anybody remembers him being angry, he never uttered a profanity stronger than "spawn of evil!" And in spite of the pistol he carried, nobody knew him to have an enemy in the Valley—or in the country, for that matter. Gus, on the other hand, was loud, outspoken and hot-tempered—always ready to pick a fight with anybody, male or female, who crossed his path: "Oh, he was a man with an awful temper, but he was a good-hearted man."[29]

Billy arrived at his homestead in the fall of 1908, and his reaction to what confronted him was that of a man faced with an impossible task: "It was very discouraging looking then, all bush or rather dense trees—like a forest and I had to clear and brake [sic] fifteen acres in three years."[30]

One survey, done in 1899 for the Dominion Government, described much of the Big Woody area as having "spruce and white birch 10" to 20" diam....the soil is of a good quality."[31] Another survey, carried out in 1904, described township 37, where Billy's land was, as "lightly undulating and...thickly covered with poplar and spruce bush from 10 to 20 inches in diameter."[32]

Most of the homesteads in the Swan River Valley, including Billy's, were called "ten dollar" homesteads—the sum a homesteader had to pay to apply for entry of 160 acres of land. It was a small fee, but as one homesteader explained,"That was the government's bet. They bet you ten dollars against you starving to death on it."[33]

Had Billy read the surveyors' reports beforehand, he might have decided to keep his ten dollars!

In those days, the homesteader used axes, adzes, oxen, fire and his own hands to clear the land. Not that Billy intended to use any of these. He planned to continue his seasonal work at the sawmills and hire someone to clear his land for him. To his disappointment, he found "everyone was too busy with his own affairs to spare the time."[34] This was a setback, but he had committed himself to the venture and was determined to see it through. At first, the going was slow and during the first two years he managed to clear only three acres of land.[35] Then, in 1911, a spring fire destroyed his shack and all his possessions, including a fine library he had amassed.[36] This fire could have been started by one of his neighbours and left to burn:

> I was amased [sic] by the eagerness of some settlers to start fires and let them run. They said,"Get the scrub cleared and get the country opened up."These fires however always [endangered] some body and besides it was burning up wood that would be usefull [sic] for fuel and for building, too.[37]

In the end, the fire was probably a blessing in disguise for Billy. He was an avid reader and the loss of his reading material seemed to give him the time and impetus he needed to "prove up" his homestead. That year he cleared seven more acres and, when he returned to his homestead in the spring of 1912, he not only rebuilt his cabin, but he was determined to clear the rest of his land: "I had my goal set on fifteen [acres] the amount necessary to get my pattent [sic]. But fifteen acres cleared in bush land, such as this, seemed a herculian [sic] task."[38]

Work progressed even slower than he had anticipated. By the end of the year he had only cleared 13 acres, 10 of which were cropped.[39] In the summer of 1913, he returned to the sawmill and, for the next two years, he hired a neighbour, Clarence Abrahamson, to clear bush and plant and harvest 13 acres of hay while he was away. In a letter dated August 15, 1914, Clarence told Billy, "The grain we sowed on your homestead did not come very well as it was to [sic] dry. I haven't had time to do any more scrubbing as I haven't had any spare time lately."[40]

Finally, by the fall of 1915, Billy had not 15, but 16 acres of land cleared! A naturalized Canadian citizen since 1911, he applied for his patent on December 15. One can only imagine how surprised he must have been when he received a letter from the Homestead inspector's office informing him that the regulations under which he had obtained entry called for the breaking of at least 30 acres:

> ...I am detailing a Homestead inspector by copy of this letter, to visit your land and furnish a report as to whether or not, in his opinion, the amount you have

broken, sixteen acres, thirteen of which are under crop, can be accepted as equivalent in the value to the required amount, if performed on more suitable land.[41]

As it turned out, Billy's efforts were rewarded. Despite his apparent misunderstanding of what was actually required, he was granted a concession "on account of the density of the scrub," and was allowed his patent on March 22, 1916.[42] It seems likely, too, that because he took eight years to "prove up" his homestead—instead of the three years stipulated in his entry—he must have applied for, and been granted, several time extensions. These concessions were not always indicative of the actual conditions of the homestead itself, however, and it was not all that uncommon for a homesteader to receive his patent without fulfilling all the requirements spelled out on the entry application. Some, such as Billy, were granted concessions and time extensions. Others were "fortunate" enough to deal with Homestead inspectors who were not above a bit of bribery:

> Well, I got my patent thanks to old Paddy MacKay. Paddy and Ed Johnson had applied for their patents the year before and they knew the ropes... [The inspector] was deaf as a post. He had one of them ear trumpets. You'd holler into it and he'd holler back and before we went in, Paddy says to me,"Now listen, he'll complain and find fault, you haven't got enough of this or enough of that,"but [Paddy] says,"He'll have his hand out," and Paddy gave me five dollars and he said,"Just lay that five dollars in it and listen to his tone change," and that's what I did and [the inspector] said, "Oh, you'll have your patent in a week."But that old bugger was supposed to come out and look at it but he never moved from Lawrence's Boarding House there.[43]

However a patent was granted, once a homesteader obtained ownership, the land was his and he could do with it what he wanted. For most settlers, their homestead was their livelihood. For Billy, who had neither the inclination nor the temperament of a homesteader, his land became simply a place for him to live. Shortly after he received his patent, he gave up farming altogether and rented his land out on a crop share basis.

1. George L.Speers,Homestead Inspector,Report #2501 on homestead of James Hamilton, 15 May 1919.
2. Interview with George Fierstine, May 1986.
3. Billy Beal's memoirs, *Big Woody*, c. 1960.
4. Interview with George Fierstine, May 1986.
5. Interview with Clifford and Edie Hanson, August 1986.
6. *Ibid.*
7. Interview with Clifford and Edie Hanson, December 1983.
8. Interview with Clifford and Edie Hanson, August 1986.

9.   Interview with Tom, Sr. and Mary Barrow, December 1983.

10. W.L.Morton, *Manitoba:A History*(Toronto and Buffalo:University of Toronto Press,1970),pp.193-194.

11. *Ibid.*,p.267.

12. *Ibid.*,p.239.

13. *Ibid.*,p.267.

14. Interview with Freda Sigurdson, May 1986.

15. Gwen Palmer and Edward Dobbyn, *Lasting Impressions: Historical Sketches of the Swan River Valley* (Swan River:Swan River Historical Society,1984),p.69.

16. *Ibid.*,p.71.

17. Winks,p.301. Winks points out that most Blacks who, as a result of these advertisements emigrated to Canada, discovered they were not welcome.

18. Beal,memoirs. Beal's memoirs consist of eight pages of reminiscences he hand-wrote when he was in his late eighties; his eyesight failing, he often misspelled—even omitted—words.

19. Minneapolis City Directories, 1900-1907.

20. Beal,memoirs.

21. *Ibid.*

22. *Ibid.*

23. *Ibid.*

24. Manitoba Natural Resources, Lands,"Application for Entry for a Homestead, a Pre-emption or a Purchased Homestead;" issued by Dominion Lands Office, Dauphin, Manitoba, 8 October 1908.

25. *Ibid.*

26. Interview with Tom, Sr. and Mary Barrow, December 1983.

27. Beal,memoirs.

28. Interview with Clifford and Edie Hanson, December 1983.

29. *Ibid.*

30. Beal,memoirs.

31. Provincial Archives of Manitoba, Notebook of J.A. Belleau,DLS. Report to Surveyor General, 1899.

32. Provincial Archives of Manitoba, Notebook of J.F. Richard,DLS. Report to Surveyor General, 1904.

33. Interview with Tom, Sr. and Mary Barrow, December 1983.

34. Beal,memoirs.

35. Manitoba Natural Resources, Lands,"Application for Homestead Patent;" issued by Dominion Lands Office, Dauphin, Manitoba, 29 February 1916.

36. Beal,memoirs.

37. *Ibid.*

38. *Ibid.*

39. Manitoba Natural Resources,"Application for Homestead Patent."

40. Letter to Mr. Beal from Clarence Abrahamson, Big Woody, Manitoba, 15 August 1914.

41. Letter to Mr. Beal from Agent, Dominion Lands Office, Dauphin, Manitoba, 11 January 1916.

42. Manitoba Natural Resources,"Application for Homestead Patent."

43. Interview with Tom, Sr. and Mary Barrow, December 1983.

Chapter Three

The Early Years

Dear Friend—I hope you will excuse me for not writing to you before... I am doing alright here [in England] so far and now soon we might have to go to France... I have been several times on pass and had all chances of good girls... Trust you are keeping well... your friend R. Root [1]

In 1914, the First World War was raging in Europe. Billy Beal, it is said, volunteered for the Medical Corps: "He wanted to join the army in the first war there—the Medical Corps—and they wouldn't let him go with the White. They were going to put him with the coloured troops, so he wouldn't go." [2]

In fact, not all overseas units were segregated. [3] This story may have grown out of one of the many rumours about Billy that were circulating—and still do circulate—throughout the Swan River Valley. Rumours that Billy may have been partially responsible for starting.

For the speculation that surrounded his early life—speculation that evolved into a kind of mystique—also encompassed his life in Big Woody. And it was often fueled by Billy himself. He revealed just enough to pique the curiosity of the people of Big Woody. Some of his comments were obviously spoken in jest: "He always said that he and Abe Hanson were the first White men settled in the Valley." [4] Still, as far-fetched as this statement was, Billy's friends and neighbours, it seems, *wanted* to believe him. Among his photographic plates, for example, there are at least five copy negatives of a light-skinned woman who was probably in her late teens or early twenties when the portrait was taken (Figure 3). Both the photographic technique used and the style of dress the young woman is wearing date the photograph circa 1860. Although those who knew Billy have not been able to positively identify the person in the photograph, many believe her to be a relative of his. And one woman

Figure 3: Daguerreotype or Ambrotype of an unidentified woman, possibly Loretta Beal. c.1860. Copy photograph by William Beal. (Courtesy of the Ole Johnson Museum.)

recalled that, years ago, Billy had shown her a photograph of a young, White woman who, he insisted, was his sister.[5]

If it seems naive that the people of the Valley would even consider it possible that he came from a White background, it becomes more plausible when certain facts about his early life are considered.

Billy's father, Charles, was born in West Virginia in 1835[6] to Samuel and Rosanna Beal. Billy's mother, Loretta, whose maiden name was Freeman, was born in Geneva, New York in 1846;[7] Freeman was a name commonly adopted by Blacks who were freed by the American Civil War (1861-1865).

Where Charles and Loretta met and when they married are not known, but on January 16, 1874, their first child, William Sylvester Alpheus Beal, was born in Chelsea, Massachusetts, near Boston.[8] On his birth certificate, no mention is made of young Billy's skin colour (Figure 4). This portion of the birth certificate was left blank only if the newborn was White. All other races were noted. This omission may simply have been an oversight by the recording clerk, or it may have been that Billy's parents' skin colour was light enough for them to pass as Whites.[9]

Billy was almost two years old when Charles moved his family to Everett, also near Boston. Here, in 1876, a second son, Theodore, was born. On his birth certificate, his skin colour is listed as "Black,"[10] suggesting that even if Charles and Loretta Beal were living as Whites prior to Billy's birth, their racial status had been changed by the time Theodore was born.

Four years later, the entire Beal family including the grandmother, Rosanna, who was widowed and living with them, were listed as "Mulatto" in the Massachusetts Census.[11] This gives us the first real indication that Billy's insistence in later years that he was of White ancestry may have some validity.

Two other children were born to Charles and Loretta: Alfred, in 1882, and a daughter, Grace Loretta, in 1885. On their birth certificates, they were listed as "Mulatto" and "African," respectively.[12]

It is interesting to note that at a time when the majority of Blacks were employed in low-paying jobs—train porters and elevator operators, for example—Charles Beal worked, at various times, as a book agent and a lecturer. These occupations must have paid quite well; he was the family's sole wage-earner and he owned his home in Everett—in what appears to have been an all-White neighbourhood.[13]

About 1891, Charles moved his family to Minneapolis. This move may have been precipitated by the deaths of his wife, Loretta, and his mother, Rosanna—both women probably died around this time although no records of their deaths could be located in either Massachusetts or Minnesota. Charles settled with his children in Hennepin County, Minneapolis, in what is today a predominantly Black neighbourhood. He found employment as a book agent and later as a salesman for a furniture company where he worked until his retirement in 1901.[14]

In 1894, Charles remarried. His second wife was an Englishwoman, Alicia, who had immigrated to the United States 20 years earlier. She was White.[15] The fact that mixed marriages were almost unheard of at the turn of the century lends further credence to the fact that Charles, at least, might have been light-skinned.

As for Billy, there is a gap in his whereabouts during the period from 1891 to 1899. He would have completed high school by this time and, if he were attending college or university, must have been enrolled at an institution outside of Boston or Minneapolis-St.Paul.[16] He may have been in Montana during these years, having once confided to a friend that he had spent some time there.[17] He also may have been in British Columbia where he spent some time working on a farm.[18]

By 1900, he was back in Minneapolis living in his father's home, but moved into his own apartment in 1902. In 1900, he was working for the Diamond Sawmill Company as an engineer. Later, he

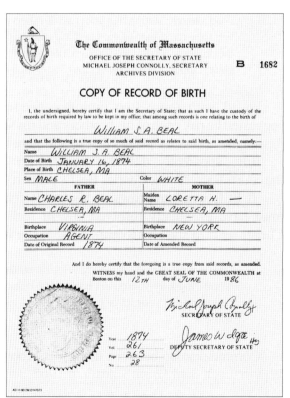

Figure 4: Facsimile of birth certificate for William Beal. (Courtesy of the Commonwealth of Massachusetts, Office of the Secretary of State.)

Chapter Four

Life in the Big Woody District

The wolves howled around the "shack" at night and every morning one could see fresh moose tracks in the snow. One shot moose then with impunity, for meat. The game wardens made no objections.[1]

When Billy Beal decided to give up farming in 1916 he did not, as many homesteaders did, pack up his belongings and return to his homeland. After he left Minneapolis in 1907, he never returned there or saw any of his family again.[2] For Billy, Big Woody had become home.

Every spring, for many years, he headed out to one of the sawmills in the area—wherever he could find work. He was, at various times, employed by the Great West Lumber Company in Greenbush, Saskatchewan, the Red Deer Lumber Company at Barrows Junction, Manitoba and Burrows Lumber Company in Bowsman, Manitoba. In the fall, he returned to his small shack on the banks of the Woody River.

As a certified steam engineer, he made a fair salary; the wages he earned allowed him to pass the winters leading the slow-paced lifestyle he seemed to enjoy. Not that Billy was lazy. Far from it. He read, pursued his hobbies and was actively involved in the affairs of his community.

There is little doubt, too, that on a more personal level he found life easier in the Swan River Valley than he had in the United States. Here, he was not confronted with the blatant racial discrimination that he—as a Black—must have come face to face with when he was growing up.[3] Still, he reportedly did encounter overt racial prejudices in his relationships with people on a few occasions.

One such incident occurred at a box social. At these gatherings, the men bid on box lunches that had been prepared by the women. Each lunch was auctioned off to the highest bidder who then shared it with the person who had made it. At one of these socials, the woman whose box lunch Billy had bought was, apparently, so embarrassed at having to share the lunch with him that she sat with her back to him "eatin' with him and they never—she never said a word and her face was red as a beet all the time... She felt embarrassed because that was something new. Like, we'd never hada dark person take part...until he started."[4]

A far more severe incident occurred in the late 1920s. At that time, the municipal road extended north from the Ditch Road only as far as the Big Woody River. Beyond that point, it was still a trail. And it passed through Billy's property. Because it was being heavily used by the lumber companies to the north and by homesteaders, Billy thought the road should be closed and the municipality forced to construct a new one away from his land. A meeting was held at the school, a vote was taken and those in attendance decided overwhelmingly to support Billy's stand to halt traffic passing through his property. The day after this vote was held, a teenager who was out for a drive came across the closed gate. When he attempted to open the gate, Billy, enforcing the mandate given to him, hit the youth's hand with a willow switch. The teenager retaliated by hitting Billy with a post, knocking him out. The R.C.M.P. were called in to investigate and one officer, upon hearing Billy's account of the incident, called him a "lying nigger." In his follow-up investigation, the policeman was unprepared for the outrage by Billy's friends which his racial slur had caused; one woman, when questioned by the officer, dared him to call *her* a"lying nigger" for backing Billy and threatened to hit him with the frying pan she was holding if he did! In the end, Billy's version of what happened was verified. He did not lay charges.[5]

Billy was also the brunt of children's teasing. They liked to call him "Curly" and sometimes made jokes about the colour of his skin. These types of comments were made innocently; the young children had never seen a Black before and were surely intrigued by Billy's physical appearance.

For the most part, the homesteaders seemed to go out of their way to avoid offending Billy:

> He used to get into square dances. We didn't want to push him aside on account of his colour. We just took him for another person, you know, and danced with him whenever he wanted to dance and he was a good-living man, you know. They all are—those people—as far as I know. They're good people.[6]

Still, prejudices are instilled at an early age and die hard. Some remarks—particularly those that made reference to his race—were probably a reflection of deep-rooted sentiments that were inadvertently voiced by parents and not meant for the ears of children. One woman recalled:

> [Billy] was at our place. [My older sister and I] were in the bedroom, and I wanted something really bad that she had and she said, "You stick your head out of the curtain and say, 'hello, nigger' to Mr. Beal", you know. So—I just barely remember this—so, I looked out and I said, "hello, niggy"... Boy, did I ever get a slap...from my mother... He wouldn't understand what I was saying, anyway, cause I was so little I wasn't talking properly.[7]

It must be remembered, though, that most of the adults living in Big Woody had themselves never interacted with a Black before, either. Their attitudes were a reflection of what *they* had been taught. These homesteaders—particularly those from Europe and North America[8]—grew up at a time when there was an unconscious acceptance of what has been called "scientific racism."[9] Thomas Henry Huxley, a noted nineteenth-century biologist and Darwinian, was certainly echoing, and perhaps lamenting, the prevailing school-of-thought when he wrote:

> It may be true that some Negroes are better than some white men; but no rational man, cognizant of the facts, believes that the average Negro is the equal, still less the superior of the average white man. And if this is true, it is simply incredible that, when all his disabilities are removed, and [the Negro] has a fair field and no favor, as well as no oppressor, he will be able to compete successfully with his bigger-brained and smaller-jawed rival, in a contest which is to be carried on by thoughts and not by bites.[10]

When Billy first moved to the Swan River Valley, then, he probably was viewed as a "romantic curiosity." And, in the early days, if the homesteaders found it difficult to accept him as an "equal," it was out of ignorance and, perhaps, fear—because he *was* different. But, they soon learned, Billy was a contradiction to everything they had been taught; he was, to them, an exception to the White concept of Black inferiority. As one resident said, "He was superior to all of us who might have been critical of his race. Not only was he superior in his education, but he was, intellectually, and perhaps even morally, superior."[11]

If Billy was perturbed by racial slights, he usually did not let on, preferring instead to shrug off—and even ignore—them: "This little girl come and looked at Billy right in his face. 'Why are you so Black?' she asked. 'Oh,' he said, 'I've been out in the sun a lot'."[12] On occasion, though, he did vent his frustration at opportunities he felt he had been denied because of the colour of his skin. He once confided to a friend that "his race had handicapped him."[13] To another friend he revealed he had wanted to become a medical doctor but "his race was against him."[14] Billy was a victim of society's attitudes and was—more than he would ever admit publicly—deeply affected by them. In 1932, for example, he wrote to the National Council of Catholic

Men asking for a transcript of a radio program he had heard "on the Catholic attitude toward the colored race." And it is only when we can imagine how powerless a man of his intelligence must have felt to be judged by the colour of his skin that we can appreciate his reluctance to embrace his racial ancestry; in 1940, when he filled out a questionnaire that asked for his racial origin, he responded: "U.S.A."[15] What must be understood—and it is possible that Billy Beal did not fully understand this—is that it was not his race which handicapped him, but racism.

Billy carried his past with him to the Swan River Valley, but here, at least, he was allowed to live with dignity and in a way which suited his temperament. He did not find a utopia but he did find a place where he could be who he wanted to be.

A doctor, for example. If, as he claimed, he was denied entrance into medical school, he nevertheless kept himself informed by reading textbooks and medical journals. And he had his own medical kit. One former resident from the area recalled Billy telling him he had taken correspondence courses in medicine.[16] And his knowledge of medicine was impressive enough that even today, many people in the Valley believe he had his medical degree: "I know he went right through medical school... His colour was against him but there wasn't a thing he didn't know about medicine."[17] There are, however, no records on file for Billy with either the Physicians and Surgeons of Manitoba or the Manitoba Medical Association; if Billy had been a licenced Medical Doctor, he would have been registered.

Even without formal training, however, the local doctor trusted Billy's knowledge and expertise enough to enlist his help in times of crises. During the winter of 1915, Dr. Edwin Bruce asked Billy to help him with the inoculation of Big Woody residents against diphtheria. Sometimes Billy worked alongside the doctor but he was often entrusted to give vaccinations on his own—Doctor Bruce going to some houses, Billy going to others. During the influenza epidemic of 1918-1919, and a smallpox outbreak in the 1920s, he was again entrusted with administering vaccines to many of the area's residents. A friend of his living in Winnipeg wrote: "I hope you have managed to escape 'The Flu' it is very prevalent here in the city. I have been inoculated twice... Uncle Fred tells me you inoculated him also."[18]

One woman, who was just a young girl when Billy was assisting Doctor Bruce, still remembers the day Billy came to her house to vaccinate her family: "I hid behind the sewing machine—he always had a little bag of homemade candy... Well, he coaxed me out and set me in a highchair and scratched my arm."[19]

Billy did not carry the sweets around just to lure frightened children out from behind sewing machines; he always had small bags of his homemade sticky, black candy in his pocket to give to the youngsters. Few things delighted him more than the smiles that small treats and surprises could bring to the faces of the boys and girls. He often bought fireworks at the annual Sports Day in Swan River and later brought them over to friends who could not afford to take their families to the event. One resident recalled:

> ...we were so goddamn hard-up—we couldn't go anywhere. We couldn't go to any of them doings and he always went in on sports days and he'd bring back a whole bunch of fireworks. Then, the next night he'd come to our place with all his fireworks... I was never home [when he arrived]... I was always workin' away. I'd come home at night and, of course, the kids were anxious about these fireworks but [Billy would say],"Oh no, wait till your dad comes home... You have to wait till it's *dawk*"... I'd set [the fireworks]...off and he'd sit back there and never even crack a smile...and whistle. But he was enjoying it.[20]

The children were as fond of Billy as he was of them: "He was remarkable with children and the children flocked to him, you know."[21] Since most came from families that were too poor to spend money on anything but the basic necessities, the treats—the candy, the fireworks—made Billy a popular figure indeed. Perhaps his greatest gift to the children, though, was his insatiable and infectious curiosity for the world around him. Because he loved to learn, he was sensitive and responsive to their natural inquisitiveness. Many have recollections of the impromptu"lessons"he gave them in astronomy (Figure 5), electronics and photography.

Adults, too, benefited from Billy's generous sharing of his talents and knowledge. Ellen Pegler, who was Big Woody School's first teacher, received lessons in photography from him. In a thank you letter, she wrote, "the lessons on [darkroom] development were very helpful. I hope sometime I shall be able to take them [photographs] myself."[22] Another resident recalled:"Intellectually, I enjoyed him a great deal, and he was a great benefit to me by his conversation... I had many talks with him."[23]

The extent of Billy's knowledge astounded those around him—"Christ, I wish I knew half as much as he did, you know"[24]—leading many to believe he was well educated. If he were well educated, the question remains: Where did he receive his schooling? There are no records of him attending colleges in either Massachusetts or

Figure 5: Mr. Beal's telescope and focusing lens. Built using stove pipe and rolled metal from tin cans. c.1930. (Courtesy of Bruce Hogg.)

Minnesota. And he himself said the opportunity for a formal education was lost to him. The opportunity to learn through books, however, was available, and it may have been through the printed page that a world was opened up to him that would otherwise not have been. His love for books—a passion that remained with him throughout his life—was probably instilled in him at an early age; his father, as a book agent and lecturer, may have been able to give young Billy books to read that covered a wide range of topics.

Billy was an avid reader. Over the years, he rebuilt the library—"a comprehensive library of learning"[25]— he had lost when his house burned down in 1911. He obtained catalogues from publishing houses and ordered dozens of books.

He spent much of his spare time sitting at home reading—everything from the books of the Bible to the scientific theorists of the day, from Shakespeare and other great classics to contemporary writings. It was probably in this way, then, that he "achieved a rather fine education in a number of fields... He spoke with authority on such subjects as philosophy, history, sociology and medicine, and, to a considerable extent, the field of astronomy."[26]

A friend tells of the time he met Billy on the road one day:

> ...I said, "Mr. Beal, I'm reading a book on astronomy and I find it a surprising fact that I didn't know, namely, that the North Star is not a fixed star, but that it goes around a great orbit of its own every 2,500 years," whereupon he said, "Oh well, George, that's right, except that it's every 25,000 years." I went home and checked the book, and it was every 25,000 years. I thought this was remarkable in view of the fact that he and I hadn't discussed the subject before.[27]

Another friend recalled, "Sometimes I'd say something to him about something—about a star—or I had to go out with him and he'd—he'd hold onto my shoulder and lean back and he could tell you every star in the sky."[28]

Billy, though, was not a braggart: "He didn't have much to say, but he was full of knowledge."[29] He was, in fact, quite the opposite—a quiet, modest man: "If he knew what you wanted to hear he'd talk... But he wasn't going to bother you listening to something he didn't know if you wanted to know about or not—you know?"[30]

Billy preferred to share his love of learning in a more unobtrusive way—by taking an active role in the development and growth of the Big Woody community. He became involved, for instance, in the formation of the Big Woody School District in 1912, was elected the first Secretary-Treasurer of the School Board and held this post almost exclusively until 1949.[31] In this capacity, he was instrumental in the creation of a circulating library within the school system.

In the early 1920s, when the Big Woody Sunday School was formed, he served as its first secretary. Billy was "a religious man" and, because he was well read, was often called upon for his interpretation of the Holy Scriptures: "I remember, particularly, when we were studying the Biblical account of the Good Samaritan that he gave a learned discourse on who is a neighbour. Such things as that linger in one's memory."[32]

Billy attended the Sunday School regularly—along with his dog, Cerberus, named after the three-headed hound which, in Greek mythology, guards the entrance to Hades. It was surely with tongue in cheek that he selected this name for the mutt. Cerberus was anything but a ferocious guard-dog. He was far more interested in stealing food from the neighbours than in protecting his master: "I met Cerberus on the road and his teeth were all stuck together—he was eatin' taffy."[33] Cerberus certainly had a mind of his own and Billy was sometimes overzealous in his punishment: "He'd get it by the tail and swing it around. They'd both be so dizzy, he'd go one way...and the dog would be walking around crooked the other way."[34]

Cerberus may have been good company for Billy, but many people remember him as a lonely man. As one long-time resident said, "Mr. Beal was so well educated that he found his life rather lonely...because he dwelt among those of us who knew so much less than he did."[35]

It is possibly for this reason that, in 1922, he played a key role in the formation of a literary society. Every two weeks, the people in the area gathered at the Big Woody School for an evening of debates, plays, poetry readings and musical concerts. He frequently participated in the debates: "He sat up at the front there and he...presided over the debates. But he took part in the debates and was quite a debater... I don't remember now what the debates were about cause they were—oh—pretty heavy stuff, some of it."[36]

Billy did not usually take part in the dramas, poetry readings and musical portions of the program, but he was a keen observer and steadfast supporter of them. There was never a problem finding participants for these presentations—Big Woody had a gold-mine of talent. Gunnar Paulson, who made up wedding songs for many of the couples in the area, was often on stage singing, or reciting a short story or poem he had written: "He'd stand on the Big Woody Bridge...and he'd look up at the moon. It was always by the moon that he'd make up all that poetry."[37] Gunnar also wrote some of the plays that the society produced. As for music, all eight Sedore sisters could play the piano and the Stevenson brothers played a variety of instruments including the mandolin, violin and fiddle.

The plays that were performed were the most popular events and Billy, as a founder and occasional secretary of the literary society, often lent his hand to their production. Around this time, drama societies were springing up throughout rural Manitoba and, in 1930, the first drama festival in the province was held in Killarney. Meanwhile, in Winnipeg, The Little Theatre began weekly broadcasts of short plays and talks on play production over CKY radio.[38] Billy must have listened to

Figure 6: Caricatures of the players of "The Bathroom Door," from the *American Magazine*. c.1930. (Courtesy of Jim and Ethel Brown.)

these programs for, in 1931, he wrote to The Little Theatre asking for information and advice on how the literary society could add professional touches to plays.[39]

The plays—which during the first years of the literary society's existence were simple "dialogues"—evolved into elaborate stage productions. Costumes were made, stage props designed and practices were held. One play, *The Bathroom Door,* was presented in several of the surrounding school districts and in the town of Swan River (Figures 6 and 7).

Billy was a man of many talents, hobbies and interests. Resourceful and creative, he utilized his knowledge of electronics and physics and became part inventor. He built his own telescope (see Figure 5) by fitting lenses onto sections of stove pipes. He made his own radio—"the first radio that was ever in that country. He bought the pieces and made it."[40] Later, when radios and automobiles became commonplace, he made electric fences for many of the farmers in the area using the discarded tubes and automobile parts.[41]

He also liked to tinker with gadgetry. Until the late 1920s when gasoline tractors began to replace steam engines that were used by the threshing crews, he was frequently asked to solve problems and make minor repairs on the equipment.[42]

One of his favourite hobbies was working with wood, and his skills as a bench-carpenter are legendary throughout the Big Woody district. His small cabin was constantly so cluttered with intricately-made desks, tables and chairs—most made for neighbours at their requests—that "he just had an alley from his door to his chair."[43] It was a situation that was further aggravated by the fact that "he wasn't too neat a housekeeper... He wasn't too particular about the corners around the house and sweepin' the floors and stuff like that."[44] Because the homesteaders had little money, they rarely paid Billy in cash. As one woman, who had Billy make a writing desk for her, recalled, "We weren't using our big victrola...so, he said he'd like to have some music, so we gave him the records and everything [in exchange for the desk]... So—anyway—he made us that desk and...he made us a birch crib. It was beautiful."[45]

He put his skills as a carpenter to work, too, for the children, making spinning tops, jack-in-the-boxes and other toys (Figure 8 a,b and c). In later years, he was often commissioned by the Big Woody School Board to do small carpentry jobs at the school.

Wandering through the district and stopping to visit with friends was another of Billy's favourite pastimes. His was a familiar figure as he strolled slowly along the road. Sometimes he walked aimlessly "communing with nature"[46] but, more often than not, he was heading over to a neighbour's house.

Billy "always wanted to visit with the women, not with the men."[47] Many was the time he could be found sitting at the kitchen table drinking coffee or tea with the wives while their husbands were working in the fields. He was content to sit for hours. Perhaps he preferred the company of women because he was single—Billy, it has been said, considered himself a"ladies' man". Or perhaps it was because, unlike most men of the day, he enjoyed discussing recipes, nutrition—even dressmaking! Dressmaking was for a time, in fact, one of his hobbies, but he seems to have given it up when none of the women would allow him a fitting. One neighbour recalled: "He was practicin' on Dora Fuson. I think he tried to measure up some of the Sedore girls, but they wouldn't have any."[48]

The women seemed to like having Billy drop by. He was interesting and he was a real gentleman. As one acquaintance recalled:

> ...he was a man of fine, old-fashioned courtesy. If he was sitting in a room and a woman entered the room, he immediately rose and then sat down again. If he was smoking his pipe and a woman came along, he immediately took the pipe out of his mouth and put   it in his pocket. He would not smoke in the presence of a woman.[49]

He was also a neat dresser, except for those rare occasions when he was working in the field: "He was always dressed as a gentleman, eh? You know how—in them days—frugal but not fancy... You wouldn't see him in a pair of ragged pants or somethin' like that to go and visit anybody—ol'—old jeans or anything like that.[50]

Billy was especially fond of visiting Louie, Gus Jonsson's wife, which, some say, was the only source of contention between the two men in all

Figure 7: Cast from the play, "The Bathroom Door":(left to right)Clifford Hanson, Dora Hanson, Jim Brown, Linda Duggleby, Clarence Abrahamson and Vi Beaumont, Big Woody district, Swan River, Manitoba. c.1930. (Courtesy of Jim and Ethel Brown.)

Figure 8a

Figure 8b

Figure 8c

Figures 8 a,b &c-: Snake in a box: when the sliding door is opened, the snake emerges and strikes! Made by Mr. Beal as a Christmas gift for Jimmy Chegwin. 1944. (Courtesy of Jimmy and Merle Chegwin.)

their years of friendship:"They were friends, but they'd get into squabbles because old Gus thought old Billy was comin' to steal Louie, and I guess he wasn't wrong, eh, cause old Beal, he was quite a ladies' man."[51] It is doubtful that Billy—who had been best man at their wedding— ever had any intentions of "stealing" Louie away from Gus. More likely, in Louie, he found someone who was, in many ways, much like himself.

Her dry wit was not lost on Billy. She, apparently, gave almost every animal on their homestead a name that began with the letter"J"—Gus, with his Swedish accent, pronounced it with a *Y* sound:"He always said it took him seven years to learn to say *yug* and then they changed it to *yar*."[52] Louie was also, like Billy, quiet-spoken, kind-hearted and someone for whom life had not been easy. But, whereas Billy seemed to be able to overcome the obstacles along the way, Louie ended her days in a mental institution in Brandon, Manitoba.

He also spent a lot of time over at the Fuson's farm. In the early 1920s, Tom Fuson, a reputed moonshiner from Kentucky, moved his family onto the quarter-section immediately north of Billy's homestead. Billy became smitten with his daughter, Dora, an accomplished pianist with a beautiful singing voice, who had been blind since birth. She was fond of him, but did not return his affections. They did, however, remain friends long after Dora married and moved away.

Billy's penchant for dropping in on his neighbours continued for as long as he was living in the Valley, although it is said that Billy spent as much time snoozing as he did talking when he visited. He could nap anywhere. In his later years, he had a habit of falling asleep in the middle of a sentence. When he awoke, he would exclaim, "Oh, pshaw, I must have dozed off,"[53] and would then continue the conversation where he had left off!

The story is told of the time he was asked, because of his training as a steam engineer, to look at a problem a neighbour was having with a steam engine. At Billy's request, a chair was brought out onto the field and set down beside the engine. Billy sat in the chair and spent the afternoon listening to the engine, smoking his pipe and dozing. At the end of the day, he stood up and without having laid a hand on the machine, told the neighbour that a piston was malfunctioning, which piston it was and how to fix it.[54]

1. Beal, memoirs.
2. Minneapolis City Directories, 1906-07.
3. Although not directed at Mr. Beal, names such as *Nigger* or *Darkie* were commonly used with black horses and dogs.
4. Interview with Lizzie Woolford, July 1986.
5. Arnold Minish, personal communication, 28 February 1987.
6. Interview with Emma Seip, July 1986.
7. Interview with Albert and Annie Daum, March 1986.
8. A 1914 rural census shows that 77% of the settlers were from England, the United States, Sweden and Germany.
9. Peter Farb, *Humankind* (Boston:Houghton Mifflin Company,1978),p.282.
10. *Ibid.*
11. Interview with George Hunt, Sr., December 1983.
12. Interview with Agnes Brauneis, July 1986.
13. Interview with George Hunt, Sr., December 1983.
14. Interview with Clifford and Edie Hanson, December 1983.
15. Questionnaire, National Stock Taking Needs National Registration, Minister of National War Services, 19 August 1940.
16. Arnold Minish, personal communication, 28 February 1987.
17. Interview with Albert and Annie Daum, March 1986.
18. Letter to Mr. Beal from Laura Richardson, Winnipeg, Manitoba, 19 December 1918.
19. Interview with Albert and Annie Daum, March 1986.
20. Interview with Clifford and Edie Hanson, December 1983.
21. Interview with C.B. Philipp, July 1986.
22. Letter to Mr. Beal from Ellen Pegler, Beaver P.O., Manitoba, 25 August 1915.
23. Interview with George Hunt, Sr., December 1983.
24. Interview with Clifford and Edie Hanson, December 1983.
25. Interview with George Hunt, Sr., December 1983.
26. *Ibid.*
27. *Ibid.*
28. Interview with Clifford and Edie Hanson, December 1983.
29. Interview with Julia Vetters, June 1986.
30. Interview with Albert and Annie Daum, March 1986.
31. Big Woody School minutes, 1949.

32. Interview with George Hunt, Sr., December 1983.

33. Interview with Albert and Annie Daum, March 1986.

34. *Ibid.*

35. Interview with George Hunt, Sr., December 1983.

36. Interview with Clifford and Edie Hanson, August 1986.

37. Interview with Julia Vetters, June 1986.

38. *Winnipeg Free Press,* 6 November 1971.

39. Letter to Mr. Beal from Mrs. John Craig, Winnipeg, Manitoba, 29 April 1931.

40. Interview with Clifford and Edie Hanson, December 1983.

41. Palmer and Dobbyn, *Lasting Impressions: Historical Sketches of the Swan River Valley*,p.203.

42. Interview with Vera Kennedy, June 1986.

43. Interview with Clifford and Edie Hanson, August 1986.

44. Interview with George Fierstine, May 1986.

45. Interview with Gertrude Chegwin, May 1986.

46. Palmer and Dobbyn, p.203.

47. Interview with Clifford and Edie Hanson, August 1986.

48. *Ibid.*

49. Interview with George Hunt, Sr., December 1983.

50. Interview with George Fierstine, May 1986.

51. Interview with Clifford and Edie Hanson, August 1986.

52. Interview with Tom, Sr. and Mary Barrow, December 1983.

53. Interview with Clifford and Edie Hanson, December 1983.

54. Arni Sigurdson, personal communication, August 1986.

Chapter Five

Photography

Dear Mr. Beal—Thank you very much indeed for the photos which reached me safely... Those of the school are especially good. You do not say what the expense is. I should like to share it, because I wanted the pictures, and the lessons on developing were very helpful.[1]

If his tenures at the lumber camps brought Billy Beal to his homestead, they also brought him to photography. In his early years in the camps, he is said to have spent at least one season in the company of Walter Barrie; a photograph taken by Mr. Barrie circa 1910—showing both Billy and his friend, Gus Jonsson—suggests that this is true. Whereas Mr. Barrie, a photographer of local renown, seemed to have supported himself partially from his photography, Billy entered into it with a zeal for the process and a love for the images themselves; he even produced a single, surviving stereograph (Figure 9).

His interest in photography peaked between the years 1915 and 1925 and there were probably few people living in the Big Woody district during that time who did not have their photograph taken by Billy; one neighbour recalled that as a youngster he was photographed by Billy in every locale in the immediate vicinity. None of his contemporaries remember ever having being asked to pay for the privilege of sitting for one of Billy's portraits. And it was a privilege—a *special occasion*—for it was one of the few opportunities they had to set aside the drudgeries and hardships of homesteading and dress up in their finest.

Today, when viewing the photographs taken by Billy Beal, it is important to remember that although he approached his craft in a professional manner, he was not a professional photographer by trade. Rather, his photographs are those of a hobbyist.

Chapter Six

Photographic Plates

I have striven not to laugh at human actions, not to weep at them, nor to hate them, but to understand them. [1]

My homestead is very difficult to clear and get under cultivation and it is very awkwardly situated as to market & c.—have some difficulties to contend with—have had some sickness in my family—one of the children died—was obliged to go to keeping a boarding house in Swan River in order to make a living but I am doing my very best to make things go.

—*William Henry Harrison Garland, Statement to Homestead Inspector—7 October 1914.*

Plate 1: The Garland children: Jasper, (front row, left to right) unidentified, Ruth and Sarah, Big Woody district, Swan River, Manitoba. c.1914. (photograph courtesy of Tom Barrow, Sr.)

[Our family] came to the Big Woody district a few years after Mr. Beal started a homestead there. His homestead was on the north side of the river, and we bought a quarter section south of the river. Mr. Beal became a very good friend of my father's. He used to visit my Dad nearly every day. They read and studied the Bible together and also went to church together. Mr. Beal always had a ready answer to give to people in church and Sunday School.

—*Letter from Mrs. Beulah Vetters—20 January 1986.*

Plate 2: Ethel and Beulah Abrahamson, Big Woody district, Swan River, Manitoba. c.1914. (photograph courtesy of Jim and Emma Taylor)

You used to thresh fairly early in them years cause you could get it in earlier, cause the land was clean. There was from 14 to 17 or 18 men [on a threshing crew], six stook wagons and probably three pitchers and an engineer and fireman—that's when they had a steam engineer. There'd be a tank man with a team hauling water. The owner of the threshing outfit would charge you so much a bushel and he'd pay his men... [You'd pay] maybe 10¢ a bushel for wheat and 8¢ for barley and probably 5¢ for oats... [You'd board the men while they worked for you] and you'd have to have the feed and water for...[the horses]. And some years when they were firin' with wood, you had to have a load or two of wood drawed up for them where they were gonna set. And the fire man—there was a fireman in that crew, too—he bucked his own wood and fired the engine.

—*Tom Barrow, Sr.—August 1986.*

Plate 3: Clarence Abrahamson standing in a field of Marquis wheat, Big Woody district, Swan River, Manitoba. c.1915. (photograph courtesy of Jim and Emma Taylor)

Well, that's my husband... I can remember that's the first little house we lived in... That's Evelyn, the oldest one, and that is Bert I'm holding... He was born in '15. That would be about that year, 1915. He's quite small there and Evelyn was two years [older]. He was [born] in '15 and she was in '13. [My husband, Percy, died in] '28. He was only 31 when he died... He took the flu and he got double pneumonia out of it, because his lungs were very weak after having the typhoid fever.
—*Emma Seip—July 1986.*

Plate 4: Percy and Emma Potten with children, Evelyn and Bert, Big Woody district, Swan River, Manitoba. 1915. (photograph courtesy of Jim and Emma Taylor)

That's Bessie Dennison. They lived about a mile and a quarter straight back of us when this was taken. She'd always meet us at the top of the hill near to where we lived to go to school with us. She got married to that old Forest Ranger who used to be up there. He used to come to our place to use the phone and when she got married, of course, they went away to Teulon... I guess that's where he'd been and she got goin' with another younger man and he sent her home.

—Lizzie Woolford—July 1986.

Plate 5: Bessie and Charlie Dennison, Big Woody district, Swan River, Manitoba. c.1914. (photograph courtesy of Jim and Emma Taylor)

That's Dora Hanson and that's her mother, Deesa... [She was a midwife] when all of us were born and she's my auntie—Gunnar's [Paulson] wife... I always wanted to be like her when I grew up... Mama was a midwife herself but Deesa brought us all into the world—her and Doctor Bruce.
—*Ethel Sigurdson—June 1986.*

[That's] my mother and Dad, Abe and Dora Hanson. My dad came here in 1901 and homesteaded and lived here until his passing... He came from the States... [He] was born in Wisconsin. My mother was born in North Dakota.
—*Clifford Hanson—December 1983.*

Plate 6: Dora Hanson and her mother, Deesa Paulson, Big Woody district, Swan River, Manitoba. c.1914. (photograph courtesy of Clifford and Edie Hanson)

Plate 7: Abe and Dora Hanson, Big Woody district, Swan River, Manitoba. c.1917. (photograph courtesy of Clifford and Edie Hanson)

It will perhaps be news to you to hear of the calamity at Bowles. He had his house burned down on Saturday night April 1st. I was there until 10.15 and he told me that at 11.30 it was about all over it seems he was sitting reading and Mrs. Bowles was in bed when he heard a crackling noise he went into the cellar to see if it was the heater but finding the fire nearly out he put on some wood and then resumed his reading. He presantly [sic] heard the noise again on going into the kitchen to see if it was the range he saw a glare on the roof of the poultry house and at once knew the roof was on fire and therefore there was no chance of saving the house he at once alarmed the ladies and carried his wife in her nightdress into the grainery [sic] and then saved what he could which was not much just bedclothes the chairs and a table they all of them lost the greater part of their wearing apparell [sic]. I believe the teacher saved all of her things it certainly is great blow for him and he as [sic] my heartfelt sympathy.

—*Letter to Mr. Beal from Fred Morgan—c.1915.*

Plate 8: Gordon (seated) and Horace Bowles, Big Woody district, Swan River, Manitoba. c.1914. (photograph courtesy of Tom Barrow, Sr.)

Plate 9: Doris Bowles, Big Woody district, Swan River, Manitoba. c.1914. (photograph courtesy of Jim and Emma Taylor)

Meeting of March 1st, 1912
A meeting of the ratepayers was held at the home of Mr. Gust Jonsson on March 1st at 2 p.m. for the purpose of forming a new school district. A petition was drawn and presented to the counsel [sic] of the municipality to form a school district comprised of, section 6 and 7 township 37,28; sect. 30 and 31 township 36,28; sect 35 and 36 township 36,29 and sect. 1,2,3,4,9,10,11,12 township 37,29. Present; Mr. C. Bowls [sic], Mr. A. Hanson, Mr. G. Jonsson, Mr. Wm. Beal, Mr. A. Abrahamson, Mr. Wm. Byron, Mr. E. Rolston, Mr. J. Chricison, Mr. J. Oliver and Mr. O. Persons.
Mr. C. Bowles chairman
Meeting adjorned
Wm. Beal, sec
—*Big Woody School minutes—1 March 1912.*

Plate 10: Big Woody School, School District #1621, Swan River, Manitoba. c.1918. (photograph courtesy of the Ole Johnson Museum)

[That's] Bob Dennison... He was a grouchin' old guy, an old English-man... I worked on the river drives with his son, Charlie...[and then there was] Bessie and Bill. Charlie, I think [is the only one still living]...Bessie died. She had a heart condition. And Bill, they said he had died, too. Bill and Charlie were out in Vancouver and Bessie lived down in the state of Washington.

—*Tom Barrow, Sr.—July 1986.*

Plate 11: Bob Dennison, Big Woody district, Swan River, Manitoba. c.1918. (photograph courtesy of George Fierstine)

[That's] Gus and Mrs. Jonsson and their horses. They're just starting to here to build on the north side of the river...pulling out logs to start their log cabin there.
—*Tom Barrow, Sr.—December 1983.*

The women liked him...oh, they liked old Billy cause he was a great talker and it was pretty lonesome up there in the bush... Gus was a worker...he was a skinny little fella...and he said,"There's Billy sittin' there in the kitchen talkin' while she's makin' pots of tea." The poor woman wanted company...and old Billy had manners, he was nice and Gus would be cross because him and his neighbours were cuttin' wood...and there was Billy a mile down the road sittin' in Gus's house drinking tea, talking with Mrs. Jonsson while Gus was with his neighbours cuttin' wood outside, freezin' and cranky as heck.
—*Agnes Brauneis—July 1986.*

Plate 12: Gus and Louie Jonsson skidding logs on their homestead with their horses, Grey and Jim, Big Woody district, Swan River, Manitoba. c.1916. (photograph courtesy of Tom Barrow, Sr.)

That's my sister, Thora, and my brother, Trygvi, and, I think, she would have been, maybe eighteen. I don't know for sure. He could have been fifteen. He was three years younger... She was wearing a velveteen dress. I think that's what they call that, with satin sorta trimming on it... [Trygvi] was a farmer... And she lived on the farm, too... She married Oscar Brandson... She died in '56—a long time ago. [My family were] all born in Canada. And we were all born here in the Valley excepting Thora. She was born in southern Manitoba where they lived first—Cypress River. My dad...was drayman there for a little while... They came from Iceland. And my mother was only eight years old when she came here... And Dad was about thirty years old, I guess, when he came here. And he had...three sons... He was married [before], you know, and she died on the ship coming over.

—*Freda Sigurdson—May 1986.*

Plate 13: Edna Sedore (left) and Freda Hrappstead, Big Woody district, Swan River, Manitoba. c.1920. (photograph courtesy of Jim and Emma Taylor)

Plate 14: Trygvi and Thora Hrappstead, Big Woody district, Swan River, Manitoba. c.1918. (photograph courtesy of Tom Barrow, Sr.)

10 Mall Plaza
Winnipeg, April 29th [1931]
My Dear Mr. Beal,

The audience should never know that there is a prompter. The prompter should attend each of the rehearsals in order to be familiar with the play and to know when a pause occurs whether it is meant for a pause or not—prompting is difficult and should be done by someone who is both sensitive and intelligent as the players have every confidence when they know they can depend on the prompter. In a three act play we usually have two (sometimes three) and they share the burden of attendance at rehearsal but always keep in mind that it is a "disgrace" to need a prompter and the prompter is there only to give them confidence and *always* out of sight of the audience.

So glad to hear your play was a success....

...Write again if you need help. Am sending you a folder about our summer school. Do you think anyone will come from Swan River?
Sincerely yours,
(Mrs. John Craig) Irene Craig
—*Letter from Mrs. John Craig of The Little Theatre, Winnipeg.*

Plate 15

Plate 16

Plate 17

Plates 15,16 and 17: Unidentified children in costume at Barrows School, Barrows, Manitoba. c.1920. (photographs courtesy of Jim and Emma Taylor)

[Gunnar Paulson would] sing at the concerts and one of us girls would play the organ for him, but he was really talented and nobody had enough brains to realize it. No, for someone who didn't have no education or anything he just could make up songs and verses like you wouldn't believe!... Charlie Hrappstead used to say,"Weren't we stupid not to remember some of those songs and have them typed out and everything," cause it was just wonderful the stuff the old bugger could remember or make up... He made up a play and we had it at the concert here, and he made up a dance and he didn't know nothin' about dancin'—made up the tune, made up the dance. He wasn't in the play himself but he picked all the things out. He picked all the characters out and we had to go to the school to practice, and it was a great long play. I was the bride. Pete Stevenson was the groom... [Gunnar] put on a wedding—like a show.
—*Annie Daum—March 1986.*

Plate 23: Tugboat "Florence Cavanaugh" towing a wanigan on Red Deer Lake, Manitoba. c.1920. (photograph courtesy of Jim and Emma Taylor)

[We'd] go to dances and things like that. We'd drive for miles and miles in the wintertime and in the summer to house parties... There'd maybe be a couple of guys who played the violin or guitar or something... [The parties would last till] four o'clock in the morning. They'd start about nine or shortly after eight, and everybody would take some lunch... [We stayed until we had to go home] and do the chores and then drive for miles [to get home].

—*Vera Kennedy—June 1986.*

Plate 25: Back row (left to right): Blanche Byron and King Sannas. Front row: Annie Byron and Julia Stevenson, Big Woody district, Swan River, Manitoba. c.1917. (photograph courtesy of Tom Barrow, Sr.)

Where I was born was Dover, Maine. I came in 1917 and my father came in 1915, then he sent for my brother, Carl, and I... He brought out...harvesters... You got your way paid out if you brought out so many harvesters... My dad and mother stayed here because he liked Winnipeg and he got a job at Eaton's. So then, he heard about all these homesteads... I guess he thought he was going to make a fortune by taking up land for $10.00 for 160 acres, so...[he] got brochures on Swan River and the Valley...and took up a homestead there in Big Woody... We came with absolutely nothing except personal [belongings]...well, my father and mother were here for two years, but as far as having any farming equipment or anything like that, we started from scratch... My dad was not really cut out to be a farmer and they only stayed the five years on the homestead, then they came back into Winnipeg and stayed one year here and then they went back to the States. But, in the meantime, I got married, and I'm still here... I was married in 1919 and then I moved to Saskatchewan with my husband and my little daughter was born there... Then, I moved back to Big Woody and we stayed another year... This is myself, and Bertha, my little girl...and these are my two half brother and sister.

—*Vera Kennedy—June 1986.*

Plate 26: Vera Leslie with her daughter Bertha(in arms) and half sister and brother, Corinna and Charles Moore, Big Woody district, Swan River Manitoba. 1922. (photograph courtesy of Tom Barrow, Sr.)

Plate 27: Corinna Moore, Big Woody district, Swan River, Manitoba. 1922. (photograph courtesy of Jim and Emma Taylor)

...and then the Sedore girls—you know the Sedore girls? They played the piano and organ... They could all pick that old piano. You bet. And they were great for dressing—dressing up...clothes meant the world to them. Beautiful clothes. Because they were beautiful lookin' girls...[Edna] had beautiful eyes, her eyes was just like a lookin' glass—they were so clear—so bright.

—*Julia Vetters—May 1986.*

We used to do the stupidest things. I remember one time Emily and I were coming home from school. We had to go right past...[Billy's] house and he wasn't home. Somebody had left groceries on his step. We went to see what his groceries were. There was a box of these great big raisins there, so we took them and eat them all the way home, and we had this empty box and we threw it in the garbage—to show you how stupid we were. And Mom said, "Where in the world did you kids get this?" Well, she made us tell...so, the next time she went to town, she got a box of these raisins and we had to take them back and tell him we stole his raisins.

—*Annie Daum—March 1986.*

Plate 28: Edna (standing), Emily (left) and Ethel Sedore, Big Woody district, Swan River, Manitoba. c.1916. (photograph courtesy of Jim and Emma Taylor)

[Billy Beal] had the first radio that was ever made in that country. He bought the pieces and made it... He made, at first, a two tube with earphones, you know, and later he put another tube on it and had a three tube one and that was the first radio I ever saw or ever heard. We used to go listen to that—Christ—sit there with them bloody earphones on till your head would ache.

—*Clifford Hanson—December 1983.*

Plate 29: Clifford (seated) and Cecil Hanson, Big Woody district, Swan River, Manitoba. c.1920. (photograph courtesy of Clifford and Edie Hanson)

There was a chap that I knew—he graded lumber in British Columbia and he came to visit me three years ago. And when I was grading lumber up there, I was getting 30¢ an hour, and...he was getting $30.00 an hour. Quite some difference, eh? Course he was...a top grader... but that's a lot of money, you know? Terrific, terrific difference... [Mr. Beal was making $135.00 a month.] Key men, that is, engineers, firemen, sawyers...millwrights and foremen—they were paid by the month. And, lesser men, they were paid x number of dollars an hour... The lowest wage up there, in the two years that I worked there, was...22 1/2¢ an hour—ten hours a day, six days a week. No coffee breaks in those days. No way. No.

—*C.B. Philipp—July 1986.*

Plate 31: Men using a jammer to load logs onto railway cars, near Red Deer Lake, Manitoba. c.1920. (photograph courtesy of Jim and Emma Taylor)

I was working at Paddock's for quite a few years. Then, when I got married, I had to work harder than ever. Cause he had a sawmill and he had two farms. I really had to work.
—*Julia Vetters—May 1986.*

It was in the fall of 1906 that one of my aquaintances [sic] asked me to spend the winter on his homestead. That was in the district that is call [sic] Lancaster now. We went out there to fix up the house and things because he had a wife to share is [sic] good fortune with him. The scrub was so dence [sic] out there that we had to climb a tree to see much of his posessions [sic]. I had originally come from the city and I thought a man must have an awfull grug [sic] against a woman to take her out in the woods like that.
—*William Beal, memoirs—c.1960.*

Plate 34: Dora Fuson, Big Woody district, Swan River, Manitoba. c.1918. (photograph courtesy of Jim and Emma Taylor)

The men would go out and work in the bush in the winter, to try and earn a little bit, and they had to leave a wife at home, of course, and they were alone, these women, for months and weeks...on end. They never saw anybody until they had one or two children and then [the children]...were too little to take anywhere to visit. Oh, the lonesomeness was terrible. In fact, some of those English brides, they went out of their minds, they really did... And the doctor would be 20 miles or so—no road to town to get to the doctor. I was born in the bush. A midwife—an old lady that went around when babies were coming. Oh, it was hard, for the women especially.

—*Agnes Brauneis—July 1986.*

Plate 35

Plate 36

Plates 35 and 36: Unidentified woman and children, probably Big Woody district, Swan River, Manitoba. c.1921. (photographs courtesy of the Ole Johnson Museum)

Dear Friend

    I am writting [sic] to ask you to do me a favour I will be able to send it Back in two weeks when Joe come's [sic] to town again. I am sending you the letter about my song. I have put one of my songs with the John T. Hall Company and it has gone in the prize contest. They send me that it is one of nine that is picked. So now I must have some-one to put music to it. If you would be so kind and not be offend [sic]. Would you lend me (10$) ten dollars for to pay for the music... if I don't act quick I may lose the only chance I have of getting one of my songs printed. I will be sure and pay you back in two weeks. If I can get that song through I can pay up all the debt [sic] we owe. Because they give a money prize to the 3 best. I don't say for sure but I might be the lucky one. Hoping you will not be offended. And let me know by return mail. Because I must let them hear from me soon.

I Remain
Your Ever
True Friend

Lillian Elizabeth Henderson

May God Bless you
Best respects from one + all

—Letter to Mr. Beal from Lillian Henderson—27 August 1914.

Plate 37: Lillian Elizabeth Henderson, Big Woody district, Swan River, Manitoba. c.1920. (photograph courtesy of Tom Barrow, Sr.)

The first week of February, nineteen hundred and sixteen, will be an important one in the history of the province of Manitoba. In that week, the amended election act will be signed by the lieutenant-governor of the province and become law. As soon as that is done, the women of the province will be citizens of the province with the right to express their opinions at elections, and with the right to sit in parliament, if the electors see fit to elect them to that important body. The work of the Political Equality league of Manitoba, as a body demand suffrage for women on the same terms as men, will have been accomplished, with the exception that women cannot occupy positions on civic government bodies.

—*Manitoba Free Press—Saturday, 29 January 1916.*

Plate 38: Thunderhill suffragettes, organized in March 1913. Back row (left to right): Mrs. Alex Muir, Mrs. Al Jackson, unidentified, Mrs. John Fawcett and Mrs. Jack Stewart. Front row (left to right): Isobelle Sproule, Linda Sproule and woman identified only as Mrs. Louie Lyons' sister, Thunderhill district, Swan River, Manitoba. c.1915. (photograph courtesy of Jim and Emma Taylor)

My mom didn't do very much. She just worked like a horse and raised eight girls. Sewed clothes for us all and knitted our socks, just like any other woman in those days, you know. And she was workin' till the day she died... She had roomers and boarders in Swan [River].
—*Annie Daum—March 1986.*

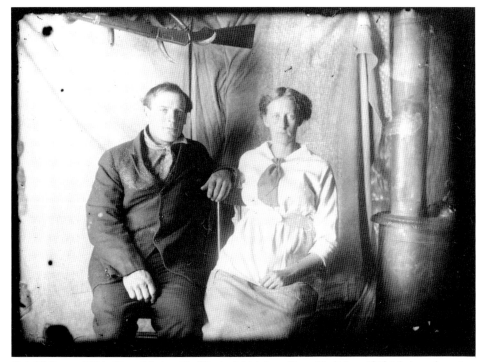

Plate 39: Roy and Hilda (Steena) Sedore, Big Woody district, Swan River, Manitoba. c.1916. (photograph courtesy of Jim and Emma Taylor)

[Gus Jonsson] used to be always rowing with his neighbours and he used to row with this old Fuson...he was a Kentucky moonshiner who moved up to this country. One time they were rowing over the line fence and Gus said, "I *yumped* that fence like an old tiger." Well, that time Fuson pulled his knife...and he says, "Gus, I aim to see the colour of your insides," and Gus *yumped* right back again.
—*Tom Barrow, Sr.—December 1983.*

[Gus] came over there and helped us one time not long before he went up north. He was over eighty then and he used to stand on his head...believe it or not. He was quite proud of this, too. He could stand on his head...and he did it to prove it, too.
—*Mary Barrow—December 1983.*

Plate 41: Gus Jonsson, Big Woody district, Swan River, Manitoba. c.1918. (photograph courtesy of Jim and Emma Taylor)

He told me a number of times that his life, he thought, had been handicapped by racial prejudice. He felt badly about that because—and well he might—because in my opinion, he was superior to all of us who might have been critical of his race. Not only was he superior in his education but he was, intellectually, and perhaps even morally, superior. He had a fine attitude towards everything excepting that he was discouraged by a long life where he thought his race had handicapped him.

—*George Hunt, Sr.—December 1983.*

Plate 42: William S.A. Beal, self-portrait, Big Woody district, Swan River, Manitoba. c.1918. (photograph courtesy of the Ole Johnson Museum)

And I remember one time my brother, Charlie, was coming up from southeast Texas on the Rock Island Rocket, and on the train he met a wealthy man from Minneapolis, and in the conversation my brother, Charles, told the Minneapolis man of Mr. Beal, who lived in a small cabin on the north bank of the Big Woody River. Charlie had also told him about the accomplishments and learning of Mr. Beal, and the man from Minneapolis said, "Well, why would a man like that live in a little cabin along the bank of the Big Woody River?" And my brother, Charlie, said to the Minneapolis man, "Can you think of a better place for a thinking man to live?" And the Minneapolis man said, after some thought—no, he couldn't.

—*George Hunt, Sr.—December 1983.*

1. Spinoza, *Tractatus Politicus 1*, iv.

Chapter heading photograph: Gus and Louie Jonsson on the bank of the Big Woody River with their dog, Bo, Big Woody district, Swan River, Manitoba. c.1918. (photograph courtesy of Clifford and Edie Hanson)

Chapter Seven

The Final Years

Yes, it's been a long and interestin' life—few troubles and a few triumphs and not much gain.[1]

When Billy Beal worked as a steam engineer at the sawmills, he was paid a good wage and earned a better salary than most of his contemporaries. In 1914, when he was employed by the Great West Lumber Company in Greenbush, Saskatchewan, for example, he was making over $80.00 a month[2]—more than double what many others were making. Billy did not become a wealthy man, however. His work was seasonal and intermittent and after 1931 his tenures at the mills stopped entirely. He had his health, though—at the age of 68, his only ailment was a hernia.[3]

To make ends meet, he learned early on to make do with only the basic necessities. Still, this did not prevent him from spending most of his money on gifts for others and in the pursuit of his hobbies. Comparatively speaking, cameras, books and woodworking tools were no less expensive in his day than they are today.

In the 1940s, he sold his homestead, and an additional 80 acres of land he owned, to Roy Sedore. Roy, who had owned a threshing outfit and sawmill, was one of the more prosperous and enterprising men in the district, but Billy did not achieve financial security from the transaction. The Depression had taken its toll and times were tough for everybody: "Nearly all the neighbours...helped one another in those days... Nobody had any money and they just more or less would go from one place to the other and help—whatever they could and so—it was one big family in a lot of ways."[4] Even Roy, better off than most, could give Billy only a partial cash payment for the land; the remainder he paid in trade goods from his general store. Billy, Roy's daughter recalled, would "get groceries...and charge them up against what Dad owed him. Instead of buying butter he'd get a pound of lard and he lived just as cheaply

Figure 12: Christmas at the Chegwin home: (left to right)Mr. Beal, the Jonsson's dog, Pat, and Gus and Louie Jonsson, Big Woody district, Swan River, Manitoba, December 25, 1946. (Courtesy of Gertrude Chegwin.)

as he could. Ten cents worth of tea and we'd have to tear a package of tea to pieces to give him ten cents worth."[5]

But even during times as tough as these, Billy did not have to worry about where he was going to get his next meal. His friends and neighbours often set a place for him at their dinner table (Figure 12): "We'd take a turkey or a couple of roosters or something and...invite him for supper. And I don't think he ate for two days before then cause, boy, he'd sure eat a big meal."[6] Nor did Billy have to worry about where he was going to live. His land transaction with Roy Sedore had been made with the "gentleman's agreement" that he be allowed to reside on the property for as long as he wanted.

Around 1950, many of the older pioneers from the Swan River Valley who had no family to look after them, began to spend the winter months at the Eventide Home in The Pas, Manitoba. The home had been opened a few years earlier in response to "a crying need for such accommodation in the north."[7] Privately run by Reverend Ralph Smith of the Gospel Mission, the Eventide Home was financed through public donations and the rent from boarders, and staffed by volunteers:

> ...up in our north there were trappers and men who had no family and no money—because that was in the days when nobody had money—so they decided—Smith was his name—Gospel Mission—he came up here and he collected—he went house to house trying to raise money and what not. He worked hard and people were very generous and got the thing done.[8]

The home, which had an infirmary, was set up like a boarding house. For about $35.00 a month, the residents were given "a warm bed and good food as well as companionship."[9] As one former volunteer recalled,"Their meals and the washing [were provided for] and if they had to go uptown for a doctor or anything and they weren't able to get there that easy we took them and they never had anything to worry about."[10]

Billy and Gus Jonsson began to room and board there during the winter of 1955. Even though both were in their late eighties, neither's disposition had changed. Of Billy, one former worker at the home said,"You wouldn't get a finer person than him."[11] And he still liked to visit with people: "I was only a couple of blocks from the Eventide. He would often come down here with his friend—the two of them. Well-mannered old fellow and polite. A very nice old man."[12] Usually, though, Billy kept to himself and passed the time sleeping or sitting quietly and reading "books that the average person wouldn't be reading."[13] Gus, still the rabble-rouser, was "great for startin' trouble. You know, getting people stirred up on somethin' that they wouldn't have even thought of. I found...he did do that to some other men... Saying they did things that they didn't do. Get two people fightin' with each other."[14]

Billy and Gus's friends visited them whenever they were in The Pas. A visit with Billy, however, was usually brief:"When we went to see him at the Eventide Home, he—he said,'Come in. We'll sit down and have a talk.' We sat down and Billy went to sleep."[15] Their friends also sent gifts of preserves and quilts as donations to the home—a practice which stopped shortly after Gus's death in 1964. Gus had made provisions in his will to have his body buried alongside his wife, Louie, in the Fairdale Cemetery in Big Woody:

> ...he had left money with [a neighbour] for his burial here, old Gus had. And so we went to the undertakers here... Well, we went there and we got [the undertaker] to phone the preacher, this Smith, and [we] had a phone, you know, you hang it up and everybody can hear it and we asked him to send the body down here. [Smith] says,"No way." He didn't either. They buried him the next day before anybody could do anything.[16]

The residents of Big Woody were angered. This anger turned to outrage when release was finally obtained to exhume Gus's remains and transport them to Big Woody; it was found he had been buried only in a rough plywood coffin.[17]

The controversy surrounding Gus's burial at The Pas continues to this day—many believe he was not even accorded the decency of a plywood coffin. One Big Woody resident recalled:

> There was great talk in those days that things that weren't right were going on at that The Pas home and even though it was led by a minister...and, I know that when they dug Mr. Jonsson up there wasn't any coffin. [He was] wrapped in blankets or something.[18]

Another friend said: "When we got him disinterred...they went up and dug him up and brought him back here. And he was, well, he was in some kind of coffin but it was just a cardboard box with cheese-cloth over it. But that's all there was."[19]

Billy, however, continued to board at the Eventide Home:"He seemed to be happy to come back for the winter."[20] For as long as he was able, though, he returned to his cabin in Big Woody when the weather warmed up and spent the summer months reading books he had borrowed from the Home's library and visiting with his friends (Figure 13). In September he would return to The Pas.

Around 1960, Billy became a permanent resident at the Eventide Home, where he remained until

Figure 13: Back row(left to right): Mr. Beal, Creth Church, Barbara Watt, Kitty Watt, Donald Watt, John Watt and Les Mitchell. Seated: Kathleen Watt and Bully. c.1952. (Courtesy of Creth and Gwen Church.)

1967. At that time, because of his deteriorating health, the staff recommended that he be transferred to a nursing home where he could receive adequate and constant medical supervision: "[He] is quite deaf... [He] leafs through books all the time but does not understand what is written (he will read books upside down without being aware of this). [He]...takes pills for his heart..is senile and confused."[21]

On September 19, he was admitted to St. Paul's Residence in The Pas. There, he seems to have spent his remaining months in relative comfort. As a long-time friend said:

> I often thought...that he wasn't as lonely as many older men would be under the circumstances. Because, in his mind, he could travel the whole world—from his knowledge of geography—and could commune with Moses and Plato and other great men of old—great thinkers—because he knew what they had said and what they had taught.[22]

Billy Beal died on January 25, 1968, in St. Anthony's Hospital. He was 94 years of age.

According to the executor of his estate, he died almost penniless.[23] Characteristic of his live-for-today attitude, it was, perhaps, fitting that there was only enough money to cover the costs of his simple burial.[24]

He lies in a cemetery in The Pas, in an unmarked grave.

> *...the human mind cannot be absolutely destroyed with the human body, but something of it remains which is eternal.*[25]

1. Interview with Tom Barrow, Sr., August 1986.
2. Letter to Mr. Beal from The Great West Lumber Company, Greenbush, Saskatchewan, 28 February 1914.
3. Questionnaire, National Stock Taking Needs National Registration, 19 August 1940.
4. Interview with Vera Kennedy, June 1986.
5. Interview with Albert and Annie Daum, March 1986.
6. *Ibid.*
7. *The Pas Herald,* 19 April 1967.
8. Interview with Agnes Brauneis, July 1986.
9. *The Pas Herald,* 19 April 1967.
10. Interview with Adi Hilton, July 1986.
11. *Ibid.*
12. Interview with Agnes Brauneis, July 1986.
13. Interview with Adi Hilton, July 1986.
14. *Ibid.*
15. Interview with Tom, Sr. and Mary Barrow, December 1983.
16. Interview with Clifford and Edie Hanson, August 1986.
17. Gordon Alderson, personal communication, 2 March 1987.
18. Interview with Gertrude Chegwin, May 1986.
19. Interview with Clifford and Edie Hanson, August 1986.
20. Interview with Adi Hilton, July 1986.
21. Mr. Beal's "Social History," St. Paul's Residence, The Pas, 1967.
22. Interview with George Hunt, Sr., December 1983.
23. Most of his possessions, which had remained in his cabin while he was staying at the Eventide Home, were donated to the Ole Johnson Museum. These include: medical bag and instruments, camera equipment, photographic plates, a home-made dry-weight scale, furniture and assorted personal papers. Some items he had given away to friends who could make use of them. These include: bench-carpentry tools, books, photographs and photographic plates, home-made telescope, toys and furniture he made.
24. Arnold Minish, personal communication, 28 February 1987.
25. Spinoza's *Ethics,* Part V

Bibliography

Baum, Willa K. *Transcribing and Editing Oral History.* Nashville: American Association for State and Local History, 1977.

Beattie, J. *John Christie Holland: Man of the Year.* Toronto: Ryerson Press, 1956.

---------- *Caring for Photographs.* New York: Time-Life, Inc., 1972.

Crawford, W. *The Keepers of the Light: A History and Working Guide to Early Photographic Processes.* New York: Morgan and Morgan, Inc., 1979.

Dobbyn, E. "Swan River Valley Logging and Sawmills." Winnipeg: Unpublished manuscript on file at Manitoba Museum of Man and Nature, n.d.

Farb, Peter. *Humankind.* Boston: Houghton Mifflin Company, 1978.

Gluek, Alvin C., Jr. *Minnesota and the Manifest Destiny of the Canadian Northwest: A Study in Canadian-American Relations.* Toronto: University of Toronto Press, 1965.

Howard, Brett. *Boston: A Social History.* New York: Hawthorn Books, Inc., 1976.

Hughes, Langston and Milton Meltzer. *A Pictorial History of the Negro in America.* (rev.) New York: Crown Publishers, Inc., 1963.

Hurt, R. Douglas. *American Farm Tools: From Hand-Power to Steam-Power.* Manhatten, Kansas: Sunflower University Press, 1982.

Johnston, Florence, ed. *80 Years in Swan River Valley.* Swan River, Manitoba: Swan River History Book Committee, 1978.

Kilian, C. *Go Do Some Great Thing: The Black Pioneers of British Columbia.* Vancouver: Douglas and McIntyre Ltd., 1978.

Lomask, Milton. *The Biographer's Craft.* New York: Harper and Row, Publishers, 1986.

McCracken, Jane, ed. *Oral History: Basic Techniques.* Winnipeg: Manitoba Museum of Man and Nature, 1974.

McGuinness, Fred. *Local History: Style Guide.* Altona, Manitoba: Friesen Printers, 1984.

---------- *Make History.* Altona: Friesen Printers, 1982.

Martin, Chester. *"Dominion Lands" Policy.* Toronto: McClelland and Stewart Limited, 1973.

Minish, Patricia and Patricia Sherrer. "Big Woody and Its Pioneers." Swan River, Manitoba: Unpublished manuscript, n.d.

Morris, D. *The Other Canadians.* Agincourt, Ontario: Methuen Publications, 1971.

Morton, W.L. *Manitoba: A History.* Toronto: University of Toronto Press, 1970; reprint ed.

Palmer, Gwen and Ed Dobbyn. *Lasting Impressions: Historical Sketches of the Swan River Valley.* Swan River, Manitoba: Swan River Historical Society, 1984.

Roucek, Joseph S. and Thomas Kiernan, eds. *The Negro Impact on Western Civilization.* New York: Philosophical Library, Inc., 1970.

---------- *Rural Survey: Swan River Valley, Manitoba.* Departments of Social Service and Evangelism of the Methodist and Presbyterian Churches, 1914.

Thomson, Colin A. *Blacks in Deep Snow: Black Pioneers in Canada.* Don Mills: J.M. Dent & Sons(Canada)Limited, 1979.

Weinstein, R. and L.Booth. *Collection, Use, and Care of Historical Photographs.* Nashville: American Association for State and Local History, 1977.

Winks, Robin W. *The Blacks in Canada: A History.* Montreal: McGill-Queen's University Press, 1977.

Interviews

Barrow, Tom Sr., and Mary (Fierstine), Swan River, Manitoba, December 1983.
Barrow, Tom Sr., Swan River, Manitoba, July 1986.
Barrow, Tom Sr., Swan River, Manitoba, August 1986.
Brauneis, Agnes, The Pas, Manitoba, July 1986.
Chegwin, Gertrude, Swan River, Manitoba, May 1986.
Daum, Albert and Annie (Sedore), Swan River, Manitoba, March 1986.
Einarson, Inga, Swan River, Manitoba, December 1983.
Fierstine, George, Swan River, Manitoba, May 1986.
Hilton, Adi, The Pas, Manitoba, July 1986.
Hanson, Clifford and Edie, Swan River, Manitoba, December 1983.
Hanson, Clifford and Edie, Swan River, Manitoba, August 1986.
Hunt, George A., Sr., Swan River, Manitoba, December 1983.
Kennedy, Vera (Moore/Leslie), Winnipeg, Manitoba, June 1986.
Philipp, C.B., Bowsman, Manitoba, July 1986.
Richardson, Teresa, The Pas, Manitoba, July 1986.
Seip, Emma (Vetters), Swan River, Manitoba, July 1986.
Sigurdson, Ethel (Sedore) and Effie Van Vogt (Sedore), Winnipeg, Manitoba, June 1986.
Sigurdson, Freda (Hrappstead), Swan River, Manitoba, May 1986.
Vetters, Julia (Stevenson), Winnipeg, Manitoba, June 1986.
Woolford, Lizzie (Vetters), Swan River, July 1986.

Suggested Reading

Blacks in Canada

Blacks in Deep Snow: Black Pioneers in Canada. Colin A.Thomson. J.M.Dent & Sons (Canada) Ltd., Don Mills, Ontario,1979.

Go Do Some Great Thing: The Black Pioneers of British Columbia. C.Kilian. Douglas and McIntyre Ltd.,1978.

John Christie Holland: Man of the Year. J.Beattie. Ryerson Press, Toronto,1956.

The Blacks in Canada: A History. Robin W. Winks. McGill-Queen's University Press, Montreal,1977.

The Other Canadians. D.Morris. Methuen Publications, Agincourt, Ontario,1971.

Manitoba History

Dominion Lands Policy. Chester Martin. McClelland and Stewart Limited, Toronto, Ontario,1973.

Manitoba: A History. W.L.Morton. University of Toronto Press, Toronto, Ontario,1970; reprint ed.

Photography

Collection, Use, and Care of Historical Photographs. R.Weinstein and L.Booth. American Association for State and Local History, Nashville,1977.

The Keepers of the Light: A History and Working Guide to Early Photographic Processes. W.Crawford. Morgan and Morgan, Inc., New York,1979.

Writing Local Histories

Local History: Style Guide. Fred McGuinness. Friesen Printers, Altona, Manitoba,1984.

Make History. Friesen Printers, Altona, Manitoba,1982.

Oral History: Basic Techniques. Jane McCracken(ed.). Manitoba Museum of Man and Nature, Winnipeg, Manitoba,1974.

The Biographer's Craft. Milton Lomask. Harper and Row, Publishers, New York,1986.

Transcribing and Editing Oral History. Willa K.Baum. American Association for State and Local History, Nashville,1977.

Acknowledgements

We would like to thank the following people for allowing us access to their collections: Tom, Sr. and Mary Barrow, Jim and Ethel Brown, Gertrude Chegwin, Jimmy and Merle Chegwin, Creth and Gwen Church, George Fierstine, Clifford and Edie Hanson, Bruce Hogg, George Hunt, Sr., Mervyn and Dorothy Minish and Jim and Emma Taylor.

We are grateful to all those who kindly set aside time and agreed to be interviewed. Their anecdotes and recollections have made this book possible. We would also like to thank the many individuals who passed along information by letter and telephone.

We appreciate the assistance we received in our research. In the United States, the New England Historic and Genealogical Society and the Minnesota Historical Society set us on the right track. Melinde Lutz Sanborn and Laura Rust provided us with information on Mr. Beal's early life. In Canada, staff at the Manitoba Archives, Manitoba Natural Resources, Manitoba Department of Education, Winnipeg Centennial Library, Ole Johnson Museum, Manitoba Museum of Man and Nature and St. Paul's Residence were most helpful.

Marc Clavet provided us with invaluable technical advice and assistance.

Chris Dugas, Rick Mitchell, Neal Putt, Z. Simon and Leigh Syms read earlier drafts of the manuscript. We would like to thank them for their comments and suggestions. O.T. Anderson, Ed Barrow, Valerie Hatten, Yolande Hogeveen, David Hopper, Peter Lambert, Shirley J.–R. Madill, Elaine Morris, Tom Morris, Linda Nelson, Marie Palmer, Rene Piche and many others were generous with their support.

We owe special thanks to Steve Prystupa for his advice and encouragement.

We gratefully acknowledge the assistance of The Explorations Program of The Canada Council.

Robert Barrow
Leigh Hambly
September 1988

About the Authors

Robert Barrow is a Manitoba photographer. Born in Swan River he has resided in Winnipeg since 1974. He has worked as a photographer for the Province of Manitoba, the University of Winnipeg and the National Film Board. His work has been exhibited across Canada and featured in several publications. He is currently staff photographer at the Manitoba Museum of Man and Nature.

Leigh Hambly is a freelance writer living in Winnipeg. Born in Marathon, Ontario, she has resided in Winnipeg since 1975. She graduated from the University of Winnipeg in 1980 with an Honours B.A. in Anthropology. She has worked as an archaeologist, copy editor and researcher.